You've Got One Shot

The Story of a Stolen Heartbeat
& What It Taught Me About
Living a Meaningful Life

Craig Schulze

You've Got One Shot: The Story Of A Stolen Heartbeat & What It Taught Me About Living a Meaningful Life © Craig Schulze 2020

www.craigschulze.com

The moral rights of Craig Schulze to be identified as the author of this work have been asserted in accordance with the Copyright Act 1968

First published in Australia 2020 by Craig Schulze

ISBN 978-0-6488067-5-2

Any opinions expressed in this work are exclusively those of the author and are not necessarily the views held or endorsed by Craig Schulze.

All rights reserved. No part of this publication may be reproduced or transmitted by any means, electronic, photocopying or otherwise, without prior written permission of the author.

Disclaimer

All the information, techniques, skills and concepts contained within this publication are of the nature of general comment only and are not in any way recommended as individual advice. The intent is to offer a variety of information to provide a wider range of choices now and in the future, recognising that we all have widely diverse circumstances and viewpoints. Should any reader choose to make use of the information herein, this is their decision, and the author and publisher/s do not assume any responsibilities whatsoever under any conditions or circumstances. The author does not take responsibility for the business, financial, personal or other success, results or fulfilment upon the readers' decision to use this information. It is recommended that the reader obtain their own independent advice.

Ethan Schulze 24-01-2014

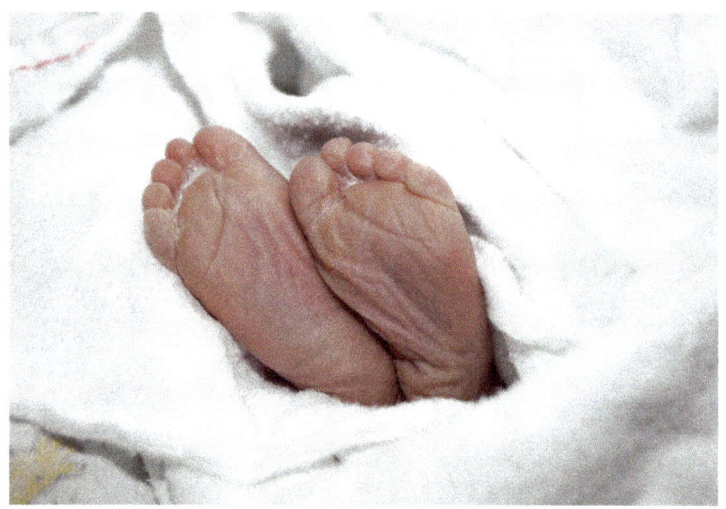

Dedicated to Ethan, my wife Karen, and my two beautiful children Zachery and Zoe – I love you.

Foreword

Challenges come to make us better. They invite us to develop parts of ourselves that are yet to be developed. Yet so often, real adversity doesn't get a chance to bare all the fruits of its potential, because we look to shortcut the grieving process. In so doing, we do not capture all of the wisdom the experience contained.

You've Got One Shot is perhaps the most honest words I have ever read as they pertain to the human experience of pain, challenge, and adversity that is all too close to home.

Craig Schulze is a seasoned entrepreneur, a battle-tested leader, but most of all a human being who has been through hell when his unborn son, Ethan, was sent to heaven. In this gripping portrayal of both Karen and Craig's journey, Craig truly digs to the depth of the human experience, showing us all what it means to continue on, when continuing on doesn't seem to be an option.

From Craig and Karen's journey arises a roadmap; one that leads us from the depths of despair to an elevated understanding of what we as human beings are truly capable of when challenge calls upon us to rise.

From moving through adversity, to overcoming ego, to developing a vision and a purpose for your life, this book not only reminds us that we have One Shot – a shot that others have not been so fortunate to receive – but gives us the hard-earned wisdom and strategies we need to make the most of it.

Perhaps the most profound wisdom that rises up out of these pages is that challenges are an instrument of evolution. They remind us how precious life is, and they invite us to become more of who we are truly meant to be. This book is a manual for undertaking one of life's most difficult yet rewarding journeys: the journey from adversity to living a life that honours the one shot we have been given.

Jack Delosa

Entrepreneur, Investor & Founder of The Entourage

Contents

Foreword vii

Introduction 1

Chapter 1: "There is no heartbeat and Karen will have to deliver your baby" 5

Chapter 2: Ethan's Ripple Effect Begins 29

Chapter 3: The Importance of Relationships 41

Chapter 4: The Journey To Connect My Mind, Body & Spirit 59

Chapter 5: Put Everything In Life Into Perspective 79

Chapter 6: How To Get The Best Out Of Your Ego 89

Chapter 7: Leverage Is A Secret To Success 105

Chapter 8: Generosity & Gratitude Changes Everything 117

Chapter 9: Your Vision is Vital to Your Success 131

Contents

Chapter 10: Take Action to Change Your Life 145

Chapter 11: Make Sure You Keep Your
　　　　　　　Dream Alive 159

Chapter 12: You Only Get One Shot at Life........171

Conclusion..181

Acknowledgements 191

About the Author....................................195

Introduction

I am not the person who inspired this book. Yes, these are my words, and this is my story. But the person who *really* inspired this book lives inside my heart, in the fondest part of my memory.

His name is Ethan, my son. Ethan is central to the greatest tragedy of my life and, importantly, the greatest triumphs. This book would not exist without him. My beautiful boy died before he was even born and that, along with the events that followed hours, days, weeks and months later, affected every year of my life since his passing.

It feels odd to say that someone who never lived taught me how to get the most from my life - but it's true. And if you let it, my story – our story – can help you squeeze every, last drop of love, gratitude, connectedness and joy from your life, too.

Life-changing events come in all shapes and sizes. Some are so significant that you know instantly that things will never be the same again. Some are so small and subtle that you don't notice their impact until much later in life. Whatever the case may be, chances are, you've experienced such a moment. The most important question that comes after that event, experience or realisation is: *what are you going to do with it?*

I set out on this journey without realising it. My life-changing moment had such a profound effect on all aspects of my life and my responses to them changed, grew and developed who I was – and am. I couldn't shake the urge to help others take that leap forward; the one that changes everything.

These moments are as ripe for opportunity as they are dangerous – in chasing growth and success and lifestyle and fulfilment, many of us end up lost in the woods without a compass or a torch. So, I feel it's more than my responsibility, it's my calling, to help others really understand, at the deepest possible level, that life is constantly offering us the opportunity to achieve our own unique versions of greatness.

It's how we learn to develop an eye for these opportunities and also how to respond to them, that makes the difference between losing and finding yourself.

In this book, you'll be taken on a journey through the valleys and peaks of my life so far, in order to learn powerful, valuable lessons and insights into how to make every day, after reading this book, count. You'll hear from prominent thinkers and inspirational figures and you'll walk away with actionable steps that you can take immediately - in order to start living your life with the passion and purpose it so richly deserves.

I know just as much as anyone that living in this world is not easy. I know what it's like to feel as if no matter what you do, you can't seem to get off the ground – or all is lost. I know that when it's difficult to see a point to everything, it's difficult to do much of anything. But I also know how to take all that difficulty and uncertainty and fear and pain and turn it into something beautiful. And special. And worthwhile.

And now I'm here to help you learn how to do the same.

Love and Gratitude,

Craig Schulze

Life Is Made Of Moments And One Moment Can Change Your Life.

1

"There is no heartbeat and Karen will have to deliver your baby"

"In the face of adversity, we have a choice. We can be bitter, or we can be better."

Caryn Sullivan, Author & Speaker

My wife Karen, red-eyed and past the point of exhaustion, wiped old tears off her face to make room for new ones. My own tears soaked the pillow beside her head.

In between us, lay our newborn baby boy. He was warm and peaceful, with his mother's nose and mouth and my hands and feet. This glorious little boy, a perfect combination of the two people who'd waited so long to meet him, in our presence, our care, and our arms, for the very first time.

… and for the last.

He died before he was even born.

My wife and I had spent all these months preparing for the arrival of our little bundle of joy. Like any other expectant couple, we spent those months reading up on pregnancy and parenting, discussing potential names and making our home newborn-friendly. In the evening, we'd sit back, relax and enjoy imagining who our child might become. I, being a sport's tragic, suggested they'd become an Olympic gold medallist (too much pressure? An AFL premiership player then?).

We were ready to do everything in our power to give our child the best possible life and present them with opportunities to fulfill their potential. As the due date approached, the anticipation was rising and the future was as bright as could be.

In the weeks leading up to the big day, Karen and I decided to take a short holiday to relax and ready ourselves for the life changes to come. Our bags were packed and all we had to do was visit the doctor for a routine check-up, then we were on our way.

Happily, the routine check-up was living up to its name. The usual stuff, there was some chit-chat… We'd had wonderful experiences with doctors, our midwife was fantastic and there'd been no issues or concerns at any stages of the pregnancy. We were dreaming of the day we would meet our child.

"There's no heartbeat, but…", our midwife's voice shattered my daydream.

But?

But what?

"…but Karen still has to deliver the baby", the midwife said.

Even before fully comprehending what that statement meant, I wanted this awful ordeal to be over - for Karen and myself. And then the questions, first and foremost: why does Karen have to deliver our baby - surely there's another way? There was no other. Unless, Karen's life was at risk, she would have to be induced and then endure the labour.

Describing my reaction to hearing those words is almost impossible, especially now, over five years since that tragic day. I remember the shock of the moment, but I can't physically feel it. I remember moving to a corner of the hospital, but I'm not sure if I staggered or stumbled, I just kind of arrived at a place.

I was no longer in my body. If I felt light-headed, or nauseous or in pain, I was too removed to notice. This must have been what people refer to as an out-of-body experience.

We stayed in the hospital that night as Karen had been moved straight into the hospital room where she was to give birth to Ethan.

The next morning before Karen was to go into labour, I was laying on the floor in her hospital room, staring up at the ceiling. My brain was in overdrive. I somehow pleaded: "I can't do this, I can't do this, please let this be a dream."

But it wasn't a dream, and it wasn't going to become one, not one I could awake from anyway, no matter how much I pleaded. This was now our reality.

It was a reality that saw months of joy and anticipation halted in the worst possible way. A reality that would force the love of my life to experience the miracle of pregnancy for the first time, through the distorted prism of giving birth to a stillborn baby. A reality that was here, now, cruel, unusual, unfair - and unavoidable.

The time had come, as we knew it would, and Karen went into labour. She displayed such courage and strength during this time. I managed to massage her, support her, something. Truth beknown my head was buried in a pillow, into which I cried tears of bitterness, pain, surrender, and agony. I'd never cried like that – I couldn't stop.

This was very unfamiliar territory for me. I'd faced adversities in my life up until that point and had learned to 'harden up' in the face of anything remotely emotional, so this unrelenting outpouring was both out of character and, perhaps, long overdue.

The midwife informed us that our child was a boy and asked us if we'd like to meet him. My first instinct was to rage against that question, as 'meeting' someone that isn't alive is… I don't know.

But once Karen and I made the decision to do so, we understood, and we are thankful to this day that we made that choice. The choice to spend time with our baby, to get to know his face, his features, his memory – and to give him a name.

Ethan.

Up until the fateful day they realised he wasn't alive, I'd always been the strong, silent type and my expressionless face – capable of giving away absolutely nothing - would not have been out of place at the final table of the World Series of Poker. During our wedding reception, speeches would include jokes about "Craig the Tin Man" (the character from *The Wizard of Oz* who was desperately searching for a heart).

I'd never even shed a tear in front of my own wife.

This isn't to say I was uncaring, but more that I kept my emotions, at best, in check and at worst, bottled up. I relied on the strong mindset that I'd cultivated over years of adversity during childhood and early-adulthood to get ahead in life. In fact, I wore it as a badge of honour. It allowed me to keep surging forward in life and in my career.

If I faced a business challenge, instead of falling to the "poor me" mindset, I'd keep it to myself and tackle it head on. I thought this was the only way that I would be able to get ahead in life. I thought that this was the true definition of resilience and that those who weren't able to do what I could do hadn't figured out how to handle adversity.

But this adversity turned my world upside down and I wasn't prepared for it.

Sign here and here

"There is no heartbeat and Karen will have to deliver your baby"

I'd signed my name thousands of times – like most of us. Agreements, arrangements, authorisations. Most of the time I've enjoyed it.

It was usually proof positive that I'd done something right: I was helping someone, achieving something, closing a deal, making a promise. A promise. We'll come back to that.

But while we're here, imagine signing a birth certificate, turning the page and then… signing a death certificate.

For the same person. A child. Your own child.

Ethan Changed My Life Forever

After going through the delivery with Karen, meeting Ethan, arranging his funeral and delivering the eulogy, something inside me changed. If this hadn't happened, chances are I would have remained laser-focused on my career and kept my personal life at an arm's length.

Ethan reminded me of the importance of connection. He helped me see that resilience and vulnerability aren't mutually exclusive and in fact, the former requires the latter. He taught me the importance of remaining present – of switching off the business mind when needs be and to truly appreciate family and friends.

He inspired me to change my attitude towards business and see the beauty in connecting with people on a personal level and sharing my story. He gave more meaning to my career and ultimately my life.

I'd never been remotely interested in anything resembling spirituality, but after all of this, I became connected to that side of being and I learned to operate from a place of love and gratitude. I'm consciously aware. I'm present. I listen. If I am about to have a tough conversation with someone, I think about where they're coming from and how they're feeling. I went from operating on auto-pilot to purposefully connecting with heart-felt intention.

Ethan's death was, without a doubt, the most challenging event of my life. While I wouldn't wish it upon anyone, it brought so many blessings with it for which I am thankful. Does my heart still hurt? So much – some days worse than others. Do I still experience flashbacks in the middle of the night? Yes. Do I wish Ethan was alive? Of course.

But in a very real way, Ethan *is* still alive. He's alive in my heart. He's alive in Karen's. He's with me on every drive to every meeting, every trip to every conference. He's a part of every step I take, every decision I make, every conversation I have and every speech I give. And he's alive in the hearts of his brother and sister.

Yes, Karen and I have since brought two healthy children into the world. They're too young to know that their father wouldn't be as attentive or involved or invested if it weren't for their brother. They're too young to understand that their brother gave their father the skills to openly express his feelings, his love, and his gratitude. One day, they'll understand that their opportunities in life didn't come only from Karen and Craig, but also from Ethan.

Ethan, my little Angel, any time I need a reminder of what matters, I look at the wallpaper on my phone - a picture of your beautiful little feet. I hope that wherever you are and whatever you are doing, you know that you have inspired, enriched, and enlightened the entire Schulze family - a family of which you have, are and will always be an integral part.

Sharing Ethan's Passing with The World

This was my initial, raw, unvarnished attempt at addressing the devastating event - Ethan's passing - on social media.

I don't remember writing it, I don't remember posting it and I don't remember noticing any reactions to it. All I know is that this was me attempting to give words to the unthinkable and writing from a heart-based place in a way that was completely new to me.

January 27, 2014

Life is a journey and is like a rollercoaster. So far, I have seen 36 years of the rollercoaster. I have had many, many highs and lots of lows.

In sport, I have reached great success winning premierships, many individual awards and having the chance to represent my state and play at a great standard of football. I have also had the lows of some heart-breaking grand final loses, injuries and missing great opportunities that have left me empty.

In business, I have had profitable businesses, I have won many awards for success, and my business has given me many opportunities. But I have experienced many challenges and growing pains of business growth.

Over the last few years, I have been blessed to inspire people all around the world. Last time I counted, I had been to over 40 different cities around the world. I have spoken on stage to thousands of people at a time. I have helped to raise money for great causes, and for those who know me, I will travel to the end of the Earth to help.

I'm a good person and deserve good things in return, but on Thursday I have been handed my biggest curveball and ultimate low of my life. My beautiful baby boy died at 31 weeks into the pregnancy. Baby Ethan Schulze didn't get the chance to come into the world and give what he has to offer.

My wife Karen and I are broken-hearted and will never be able to get over this loss. But over the last few days of devastation Ethan has already made me a better person. I have learned how to open my heart, I know that I cannot take anything for granted, I am now hungrier for success and Ethan will be my power, my force, and my angel that takes me to the top.

I want to make him proud and he is my WHY in life. Ethan is the reason for me to keep moving forward to live every day to the fullest. If you are one of the lucky ones to have little ones in your life, give them a big hug and appreciate what you have.

Holding Ethan after birth was a moment to treasure forever. It took me to a place of emotion I had never been before. I spent over 10 minutes promising him of everything I was going to do in life to make him proud and that he will be watching me saying, "That is my Dad."

When I was holding him, he looked peaceful. He had my hands and feet, Karen's nose and mouth and my dark brown hair. He also had his tongue poking out and a tear in his eyes. I know he would have had my drive for success and Karen's warm loving heart. The two days we were able to spend with him were short, but his presence made me feel the power and inspiration.

So, moving forward. It is tough and going to be a long road. But Ethan has already given me more inspiration and made me a better person and changed my perspective on life. I know he will be above to protect me and guide me in the right direction and I feel safe knowing he will be around. In the challenging times ahead, I will look at his beautiful feet and his name which is etched on the inside of my wedding ring.

So, the message is this. Live life to the fullest, do not worry be happy, do not let the small things get in the way and challenge yourself to achieve great things. But, most importantly, if you have kids make them your treasure of life.

Love to all.

Every year since Ethan's passing, I have taken time to write of our connection, my hopes, dreams and what might have been for him and for us, as a family. I call it a tribute, thanking him for the inspiration, the love and vulnerability and the ability to feel - everything.

I will be sharing these annual tributes throughout this book in the belief that it will frame some of the lessons I've learned and, at the same time, help complete a picture of what may be possible for you when you explore your own heart - and follow it.

Ethan's Eulogy

Barely a week on from this tragedy and from within a haze of grief, I found myself speaking these words in the form of a eulogy at our first-born son's funeral – a sentence that still to this day, is difficult to type. It is during this speech that I made the most significant of promises to Ethan, to Karen, to the congregation and in a sense, to the entire world.

> For starters, I have to thank everyone for coming.
>
> The shock of Ethan's passing has been a curveball from nowhere. Karen and I were not sure what to do in regards to this service whether to just be us, our family, but since that day we have had unbelievable support from everyone in our network and we knew it was right to open it up to anyone who wanted to show their support. So, we say thank you so much for your support.
>
> This is the hardest thing I have ever had to do. At Christmas time, I was in the most perfect place in my life. I was surrounded by family and friends having great laughs, and as I sat

there watching all my beautiful nieces and nephews running around, I thought 2014 is the start of a new journey. 2014 was in my mind and mapped out already. Karen had the sparkle in her eyes, and you could see she was ready to become a mother, but one month on, our world has been tipped upside down.

So, here we are one month later burying our son, being left empty inside, asking questions as to why us, why has this happened, why Ethan, why now? So, we are calling this a tribute as we have no journey to celebrate just sadness that Ethan did not have the chance to give what he had to give. I know Ethan would have been the complete package carrying my drive and hunger for success and Karen's beautiful warm loving heart.

So, here we go. I am going to apologise in advance for my emotion, in Karen and my relationship of seven years she had barely seen me shed a tear. Since the 24th of January, I have shed enough tears to last a lifetime. So, Ethan has already made an impact. I can dig deep into my emotions and let it all out.

Trying to draw positives are the things I have thought of a lot lately and that Ethan has been the gift of power with the purpose to make me a better person, to make me cherish life and to value every minute. I have also thought that maybe Ethan's purpose is that he needs to help me, protect me, and guide me through life. I have asked all the questions to why, but all I come up with is there has to be reason for Ethan. I already know I am a better person from Ethan's presence.

I want to share with you this experience as this moment changed our life.

Karen, I love you and your bravery gives me strength. I can clearly remember Karen's face when the midwife was saying "Craig, there is no heartbeat, but she has to deliver the baby".

I felt sick in the stomach and could not fathom Karen having to go through labour knowing the outcome. It was the most emotional feeling I have ever felt in my life. I was thinking I cannot go through with this, I cannot see our baby in this situation and I do not want to start this journey again. But guess what, we had to do it. We had no choice, it was not a dream, it was reality and we had to go through this experience.

So, the time comes, and Karen went into labour. I was trying to support and massage her, but I was an emotional wreck where my head was buried in the pillow completely shattered while massaging her.

Then I hear the voice of the midwife, "It is a little boy". I was looking at Karen in amazement and thinking I do not know how you did that, I thought you are superhuman to go through that experience.

The midwife asked, "Do you want to meet your baby?" and I was very emotional and unsure as I was not sure if I could have my memory of Ethan as a sad one. Karen wanted to see him, and she held our baby. I sat there in the chair and I knew it was right that I had to meet him.

Our baby was just beautiful. He was warm, he looked peaceful, he had my hands and feet and Karen's nose and mouth. But when I was holding him, there was a tear running down his face. Karen said straight away, "I think he looks like an Ethan," so we named him Ethan Schulze.

Over the next two days, we had a special time with Ethan. I have a beautiful photo of Ethan in Karen's arms while they are asleep together. We have some memories of Ethan spending precious time with his proud grandfather Harry, and loving Aunty Leanne, meanwhile Pauline (Karen's mum) needed to support her parents across the other side of the world and my family had to provide me with comfort over the phone.

We had the chance to have him blessed, which was a moment of empowerment for us as parents. After the blessing, I held Ethan and looked at him and, as I cried, I promised him everything I do in life will make him proud. I asked Ethan to promise me that he would guide me, help me, support me and protect me because I won't be able to get there without him. As Karen and I sat in the room with Harry and Leanne, we were speechless and together we could feel his presence.

When the time came to say goodbye to Ethan, as soon as he left the room, we had an empty feeling. So, those two days are my memories that I will cherish forever. When I think of those days, I feel empowered and inspired to move forward. I feel Ethan's spirit is around me and I feel comfort that he is watching me. He is my Angel.

So, now my dream in life and what live for now is to have a beautiful healthy family where my children grow up one day and achieve great success in whatever their chosen field. In my dream, I can clearly visualise the moment where Karen and I are sitting in the crowd at the Olympic games or the Australian Open or the AFL grand final with tears in our eyes as our son or daughter gets up on the winning post and, in their speech, they acknowledge everyone.

But, at the end of the speech they say, "But finally, the reason I am here today and the reason I have dug deep and put in all the hard work is for my older brother Ethan. My older brother has inspired me to be here today. He was not given the chance to give what he had to offer on this Earth, so he has been my inspiration to succeed". That is my dream and it makes me smile.

Karen and I have got a long, long way to go to get to that point, but that is now my WHY in life. It will get me out of bed in the morning day after day until that happens. We want to thank everyone for all the messages, gifts, flowers, meals, friendly catch ups and support in general. In times like this, family and friendship is required to help you pull through.

In my lasting words to Ethan. I was the happiest man on planet Earth until January 24th. Every night, Karen would go to bed and I would kiss her tummy and say, "You are gunna be a sports star". I loved you so much.

So, I am left empty that you will not be able to make your mark and give all your talents to make this world a better place. You would have been proud to have us as parents. You would have been loved, cared for, looked after and treated like royalty. Maybe it is just that I could not do it alone and needed your guidance which is why this has happened. We will never know.

But one thing I will promise is this. You will be proud of your dad, because I will do great things that will amaze you and you will say, "That is my dad." Ethan, the one thing I will ask of you is that you can look after us, protect us, and make sure we are guided in the right direction and give us healthy happy brothers and sisters. You have already made a huge impact in such a short time. I will love you every day, until one day we meet again.

On a brighter note, I want to share with you Ethan Schulze's impact already.

ETHANS IMPACT ALREADY

The day he was born was the day my gym contract with the hospital was extended. I have been waiting for that for months and months and Ethan gets it done straight away.

Ethan has already made me cry more in one week than in 36 years.

Much to Karen's delight, I now wear my wedding ring every day. I normally only wear my wedding ring socially. I have Ethan's name scribed into it now.

On my birthday, it was Australia Day and we could not find a car park within 1km of the venue we were going. But sure enough, a car pulls out right outside the front of the building.

I will be a good dad, but I think Ethan has made me appreciate and value life and family more than I already did.

Ethan has provided me with a feeling of power and inspiration.

So, Ethan you have done a lot in such a small time. You will no doubt make a major impact in the future.

Life is made of moments and one moment can change your life. Losing Ethan was one of those moments for me. From that moment on, my vision and mission for life was fuelled by passion, purpose, and a desire to make an impact and leave a legacy.

"There is no heartbeat and Karen will have to deliver your baby"

Your One Shot Lessons

The tragedy of losing my son awakened me to too many universal truths to name. Here are a few:

- There are moments in life from which you will feel nothing positive can be gained, but they will completely change the way you look at the world. Eventually, you'll be stronger, kinder and/or better for it.
- Remaining hyper-focused on rigidly-set goals and ignoring the present moment may well hurt you in the long run.
- Being hardened-up, 100% stoic and unbreakable doesn't equal being strong.

Be Present And Consciously Aware Of Every Moment In Time.

2

Ethan's Ripple Effect Begins

> *"From the sadness, learn something; from the happiness, learn something. From the setback, learn something and even from the success, learn something. Never stop learning from any situation in life, for that is where the wisdom lies."*
>
> **Gift Gugu Mona, South African poet**

After three straight days of something akin to anguish taking root in the pit of my stomach – a seed of something new, very different, was taking root. It was a speck of light within the darkness. It was a feeling of purpose that led to a promise.

You'd think that after losing a son and spending two days at the hospital grieving his love even while he lay lifeless in your arms, you just couldn't contemplate any future fatherhood for a long, long time. You would be forgiven for swearing off dreams of parenting and letting grief really take hold.

Grief, of course, was to come, but in that moment in time, as I signed both a birth and death certificate within the same hour of the same day. I experienced what can only be called an awakening.

"Ethan, while we have no choice but to part ways, know this: your passing will not be in vain. I promise you that from this moment on, I will do everything in my power to carry forth your legacy. Your mother and I will have a little boy or girl, your brother or sister, and we will give them everything that we would have given you.

I will be the best father that I can be. I will make an impact on this world and give you something of which to be proud. I will work as hard as I can for the sake of our family, but I'll never let that work take away from what's important – being present for your mother and your siblings. With every fibre of my being, I make this promise to you."

That day, in that hospital, I said goodbye to Ethan, at least for the time being. Walking away from the experience, I wasn't the same man… I was different and I'd never look at life the same way again.

You've Got to Start Somewhere

Queenstown, Tasmania, 1991. 8:00AM.

I clicked my Stack Hat into place and leapt onto my trusty BMX. With a stomach full of breakfast cereal and adventure in my veins, I sped off into the belly of Queenstown. One BMX was joined by a handful of others and my tight-knit group of energetic youngsters took a break at the local lake.

The day was full, jampacked with activity. Swimming, fishing, basketball, a spot of footy. When zipping past any of the few thousand Queenstown residents, we were met with friendly faces and, to tell you the truth, I can't remember it ever being any other way.

As the sun went down, my mates and I were still at it. When my parents noticed that it was after 8:00pm and I still hadn't returned home, they didn't bat an eyelid. Eventually, they heard the shuffling of my tired feet and saw my dirty knees and happy but worn-out face. A plate of dinner was waiting and sleep was on the horizon. That was a good day, and happily, there were many like it.

Apart from the names and places and maybe even a couple of the activities, this might be a familiar story or recollection for many of you or even the people you know. That was then and this is now, though. In any case, I was lucky enough to grow up in a great town full of great people. Queenstown was a mining hotspot and was made up of decent residents with decent ways of looking at life.

I came from a close and loving family and benefited from dedicated, hardworking parents who gave my siblings and I all that they could give us. They nurtured and brought out in me a strength of character that included respecting others and myself. It was a safe, happy childhood and I wouldn't change anything about it.

However, Queenstown was isolated. It was a place that offered richness and fulfilment for some but not much in the way of opportunity. For many years, I operated under the assumption that everyone was exactly like the residents of my town.

If I wanted somewhere to channel my considerable sporting talents, my father was forced to drive me way out of the area. And lucky for me, he did – multiple times a week. If I wanted to progress further than year 10 and complete the final two years of high school, I had to travel three hours out of town. At the age of 15, I had no choice but to branch out.

I've given this brief overview of my upbringing to highlight the fact that thanks to my parents, I would have been a good father regardless of whether or not the experience with Ethan had taken place. I am forever grateful to both my mother and father for doing everything in their power to ensure we grew up the right way – with character and conviction.

But prior to Ethan, I looked at life through black and white lenses. I believed that we all followed the same, standardised path, which went something like this:

1. Get a good education
2. Secure solid employment, possibly with some room for growth
3. Get married
4. Have children
5. Buy a house
6. Invest, maybe get a share portfolio
7. Slowly build a retirement nest egg and you know the rest

No matter where I was or what I was doing, I was constantly consumed by where I was on this path. It might sound old-fashioned now, but a lot has changed about how we all view life today. In any case, I made sure that I was always moving forward but within this rigid blueprint, to the point that I grew uneasy if I wasn't sticking to it.

Ethan changed all of that.

The Father I Am Today

In those weeks after leaving the hospital, that awakening hadn't faded. Yes, my wife and I were grieving. No, we weren't out of the woods yet (nowhere near to be honest). But that promise I had made to Ethan wasn't a flash in the pan nor an example of being a prisoner of the moment. I was looking at everything around me with new, refreshed eyes.

My emotions weren't buried. They were on the surface, exposed, and they were amplified. I wasn't spending most of my time worrying about what was coming next, but I was present in a way I never had been before. In other words, for the first time in my life, I was consciously aware.

It was during this time that I made my first notes on what has now become this book.

This new mindset and way of being carried me forward. It was with me when Karen, once again, fell pregnant. It was with me through the birth of our son, Zachery, and again through the birth of our daughter, Zoe. For so long, the future was a series of markers to be reached, that would in turn tell me that I was progressing, in step with that blueprint I mentioned. Now, the future was a means for me to honour the life that Ethan was never able to live.

Before Ethan, I would have worked to help develop in my children the same life tools (such as planning, focusing on achieving goals, respect for others and themselves) that were developed in me, by my own parents. After Ethan, I realised that this wasn't a 'by-the-numbers' process. It required presence. It required a deep sense of living and staying in the moment. Now, if I'm working from home and my children approach me with play on their minds, I don't let my achievement mindset shut them out.

Instead, I achieve something more special: the keeping of a promise to a special young boy and time spent with my precious kids. I go with the moment and take advantage of the time I get to be a father to young children.

Time with my family isn't calculated or schematic. It isn't dictated by preconceived notions of how to raise grounded or successful children. Fatherhood is now a live, natural process formed by true connection. I'm emotionally invested.

I'm consciously aware of every second, every minute and every hour that I'm lucky enough to spend shaping who they are as individuals. I make sure that I open their eyes to this incredible world and what it has to offer. I want them to fight for their dreams and live a life of passion and purpose. I think everyone should want that – for themselves and others they can care about.

I have a recurring daydream. That one day, I'll be sitting in the audience of some kind of awards ceremony – however small in scale. It could be an end-of-year school event, it could be during the aftermath of a local sporting season, or hey, it could be after the AFL Grand Final (a father can dream!).

The event isn't important. But what I would love to see one day, is either of my children celebrating some form of achievement, by paying tribute to the brother they never met. They'd say something like, "My big brother didn't get his one shot at life, but because of that, he's inspired me to do what I've done today".

Of course, it doesn't bother me in the slightest if this doesn't happen. But when my mind is overloaded with everything that needs to be done, I can calm myself with this thought. I suppose, in some ways, Ethan didn't die – he just didn't get to live.

But he lives with me in those quiet moments.

Your One Shot Lessons

I happened to learn the following through tragedy, but anyone who has ever been successful has learned the same lessons at one point or another.

- Too often, we are taught to live life according to a universal blueprint, following steps that must be taken in the right order. This is restrictive, unhealthy and just plain wrong.

- There is no single, precise formula to living a successful life because success means something different to everyone.

- Being consciously aware allows you to shake off the shackles of expectation and truly live in the present moment.

A Letter to Ethan

January 24, 2015

Today is Ethan's first birthday. It is amazing to think how time flies. This time one year ago, my life was changed forever. Losing Ethan was easily the hardest day of my life.

His spirit will always live on and the value and joy he has provided Karen and myself is amazing.

He is now my guiding angel and had such an amazing impact on my last 12 months.

He will be in our hearts forever.

RIP little man, until we meet again.

Focus On Building Meaningful Relationships.

3

The Importance of Relationships

"Our wealth is rewarded in direct proportion to the number of people with whom we are willing to share."

Paul Zane Pilzer, Author of The Next Millionaires

Karen and I pulled up to the driveway of our home, as if it was any other day. But it wasn't. We had just arrived home from the hospital – without Ethan.

Our house, usually a symbol of safety and security, of the all dreams we've had and will have, now seemed lonely - a place of incompatible purpose, fit for a newborn that never came. To be honest, our first impulse was to remain in the car, to avoid crossing the threshold into the hallway where all that awaited was a bitter reality and an empty cot. But somehow, despite ourselves, we made our way inside.

Here we were… at home.

I expected to feel like the quiet would kill me. For the new emptiness to swallow me whole. Instead, I noticed an overwhelming wave of strange scents. It was confusing, as this was not how our home usually smelled. We followed our noses into the house and one look at the living room froze us in our tracks. The entire space was so entirely jampacked with various types of flowers that the walls were no longer visible; condolences, without beginning or end, that instantly shone a comforting beam of light right at the heart of our darkest moments.

Then there were the cards - such kind, thoughtful, wonderful words. Each one making our house feel less and less stark. Some from our closest friends, some from people I hadn't seen in a decade. Barely a few days later, Karen and I were startled by a knock at the door. Upon answering it, there was no one there, just a gorgeous looking box sat on the welcome mat.

Carting it inside and prying it open revealed a treasure trove full of beautiful keepsakes and incredible gifts. We sat on the couch, crying and laughing, our hearts overflowing with sentiment. It turns out that my sister Lisa had encountered a friend who made keepsake boxes for those who may have been through tragedies similar to ours.

The box and its contents are still to this day one of our most prized and meaningful possessions.

And then there were the conversations – friends and family visited and sat down and listened with empathy and we engaged in some of the deepest, most meaningful conversations I've ever had. Little Ethan had brought together everyone in our lives and reminded us of how loved we were. How lucky we were to be loved with such generosity and sincerity.

This would never have happened if I hadn't learned the importance of meaningful relationships and now, I was getting to know the full meaning. The other side of relationships. The side that extends a hand, a thought, a kind word, a deed when you simply can't make it by yourself.

Meaningful Relationships Are Worth Their Weight In Gold

I found myself re-examining relationships and the concept of relationships with fresh eyes – through the lens of grief, introspection and eventually, with a deeper understanding. Relationships are not something that you can value or participate in on a part-time or casual basis. If you want relationships to last, you're either all in or you're all out. Being who I am, I tend to breakdown challenges, projects and goals into steps. And because I truly wanted to honour everything that Ethan's legacy gifted me, I decided to consciously embrace all aspects of building, establishing and nurturing relationships, paying particular attention to the path I took. It's what life is all about.

I learned a lot just by being more aware, more present and more appreciative. But I also made some interesting observations that you may find worth considering in your own life. What I don't want to do is spit catchphrases and clichés at you, because while they're easy to remember, many of them don't actually help you strengthen meaningful relationships. But, if you listen to enough people, keep an open mind and read and absorb enough wisdom, you'll sort the wheat from the chaff – you'll realise what's real and helpful in both your personal and business life and what isn't.

For instance: "your currency is your contact list" and "your network is your net worth" both highlight how much success lies in the people around you. The more you can show yourself to be a worthy comrade in life and in business for that matter, the more people will value you and your uniqueness – and the better you'll fare in all areas of your life.

Another worthwhile philosophy is to ensure that the people around you bring out the best in you and vice versa. You've probably heard that old saying that if you look at the five people with whom you spend the most time, you'll realise that you're mirroring their attitudes, behaviours and perspectives (if you already haven't).

So, if you're hanging around people who have zero interest in growing and moving forward in life, there's a good chance that you'll end up sharing their attitude – and the "rewards" that come with it.

American author Zig Ziglar said: "you can get everything in life you want if you will just help enough other people get what they want." These words embody the mutually beneficial aspect of meaningful relationships.

Developing Meaningful Relationships

In life, I don't think there's as strong a guiding principle as harnessing the power of cultivating meaningful relationships. Without it, I wouldn't be the husband, father, son, friend or entrepreneur I am today.

Experience has taught me a lot about relationship-building with respect and sincerity. I've also made some observations on how *not* to build solid relationships. Again, these are simply my observations around sometimes well-meaning but often ineffectual approaches toward relationships -things to look out for.

1. **"I can do it all myself"** – no person who has ever achieved success has ever done it without the help, support or guidance of other people. You know it and deep down, most other people do too. In this hyper-competitive world, many are tempted to keep all their eggs in their own basket, mistaking self-belief and autonomy for never needing anyone but the person in the mirror. Whether it be a mentor, a partner, a friend or even someone who inadvertently said something that resonated with you, we all need others in some way, shape or form.
2. **"I churn and burn"** –the flipside of the coin is the belief that other people exist purely as a means to an end. I have seen this too

many times – and maybe you have too. I'm talking about those who befriend others for cynical reasons and extract all that they can before walking away/losing interest/seeing something (or someone) better, eventually realise what it has cost them – a chance at a genuine relationship. Sure, there are many extremely successful people who have climbed the ladder by using others then burning bridges but, more often than not, these people end up alone with not much more than regret. There's no way you can achieve *true* holistic success in life with this mentality.

3. **"Everyone has to like me"** – in an ideal world, everyone would prop each other up and be genuinely invested in each other's happiness. The harsh truth is that others can bring you down and get in the way of you fulfilling your potential and living your most genuine life. Hey, they might not mean to, but it happens. People who view everything through a negative or destructive lens can severely impact your own attitudes and while I'm not saying that in all cases you should cut them off, you shouldn't work to maintain a relationship if you're doing so purely to

please the other party, especially if it's to your own detriment.

The overriding point is that we should all, at some stage in our lives, assess how we relate to other people - be brutally honest with yourself. If you're falling into any of the above traps, take a step back and take what may be your only opportunity to step into your relationships with fresh eyes and an open heart.

It sounds a bit sentimental until you ask yourself: how many lives do I have and how many chances to build genuine relationships will I get?

Trust, Like & Respect

I owe my perspective on building, and yes, enjoying genuine relationships to a number of people. Firstly, my parents, who instilled in me a general foundation of decency. And to one of my clients – a member of the first business I owned – a local gym.

This member ushered me into the world of entrepreneurship and introduced me to a number of philosophies I still stand by to this day (including leverage, which is a topic that

I'll explore on a deeper level later in the book). Either way, on an emotional, philosophical, and yes, commercial level, I have benefited from investing in people who I like, trust and respect.

In 2003, amongst the first group of gym clients, I, the novice business owner, met with a lovely semi-retired professional couple, Rob and Jo. They were a fantastic pair and we hit it off in an instant. As my family lived in a different state, this couple, over time, became my surrogate parents, inviting me around for dinner after finishing work of an evening, or getting together over the weekend to chat about anything and everything for hours on end.

After more than 15 years of a close bond – involving chatting on the phone and catching up in person wherever possible – these firm friends were even firmer fixtures at my wedding. A couple of years ago, we attempted to meet up in Singapore but passed like ships in the night although I'm pleased to say that the connection is alive and strong and will never break. From the beginning, both parties approached our connection with an open heart, and I am blessed with lifelong friends who'd do anything for me, just as I would for them.

Tip: the trust, like and respect model, if you want to call it that, ignores age, position in life, allegiances to footy teams and just focuses on values. Do we value and respect the same type of things and each other? That's the question.

Create Value In Your Relationships

I use the example of Rob and Jo in the previous section, to show you the importance of investing in what you value. I valued their kindness and perspectives and took the time to maintain the friendship and I'm a better man for it. Relationships aren't transactions and if you go into any connection with expectations of receiving something in return, it will not last. Instead, put as much as you can into a relationship.

In my downtime, instead of watching TV for hours on end, I act on the conscious decision to call people who I trust, like and respect in order to catch up, see how they're going and therefore keep the friendship alive.

This practice has proven invaluable to me. It has helped me feel a part of a network of care and support and ensured that I never feel as if there's nobody I can turn to. Relationships aren't a one-way street, so if you feel as if your friends have all stopped caring or that you're more alone than you've been in the past, perhaps you haven't been investing in meaningful connections. Perhaps you still can.

Now to the sticky part. A by-product of cultivating meaningful relationships is that they can help you in your pursuit of success. Before I continue down this line, I need to make it completely clear that I am by no means promoting assessing the worth of relationships based on whether or not you can benefit from them – far from it.

I'm just saying that if you genuinely like, respect and trust a person, in time, doing all that you can to help each other comes naturally. The relationship always comes first and propping each other up is a natural result of that mutual respect and goodwill.

For example, due to my honest, sincere approach to flagging any business that I felt deserved more clientele and then referring it in the most organic fashion, local cafes and restaurants in my home area have generated increases somewhere between $10,000 and $100,000. The by-product of this process is that the owners of those businesses would name-drop my gyms whenever it felt right.

To be completely honest, my first gym was mostly built on referrals. However, relationships mean far more than mere numbers in dollar terms. The important and lasting legacy of a relationship is connection and I've found it valuable to think about each of these connections as having one of three key characteristics.

The 33% Principle

A good friend of mine once introduced me to an interesting way of assessing the relationships in your life. Now, once again, this is in no way prescriptive, but it is symbolic of what it may take to live a full, well-rounded and forward-moving life. It goes something like this:

- 33% of your relationships should be with people who **share your mindset**, largely your true 'life' network (friends, family, business networks, leisure groups).
- 33% of your relationships should be with those **who can help you drive forward**. Those that inspire, advise, challenge and facilitate growth (mentors, senior colleagues)
- 33% of your relationships should be with those who you are able to help in some way,

shape or form. People who look up to you for guidance in order to move forward.

I'm not suggesting that you look at your relationships and begin a process of adding and culling until you reach this balance. I'm also not suggesting that you view the people in your life solely through how successful they are in comparison to yourself. This rule is more of a guide and focuses on realising and balancing the importance of three types of people: those you look up to, those who you relate to and those that you can help.

Thirdly, this by no means suggests that if anyone you know doesn't fall into any of these categories, that you should delete their contact details and pretend you're not home if they knock on your door. Variety is the spice of life, so different opinions are great.

But what about that friend or family member who tends to put a negative spin on everything? Well, maintaining that connection is fine and admirable. But by the same token, it's imperative that you don't let their attitude negatively impact yours. That leads to lost opportunities and dissatisfaction. And you don't need that.

Generational Wisdom: Teach Them Well

My kids are both too young to consider the worth of other people, but as soon as they are old enough, I will ensure that they understand that cultivating meaningful relationships and doing so from a genuine, heart-based place is one of the primary foundations of a successful life.

The benefits of this understanding are many and include:

- A feeling of connectedness and inclusion
- Support and companionship through the good times and the bad
- A means to explore, discuss, clarify and problem solve
- Increased purpose – living not just for yourself but for others
- The ability for two parties to help each other grow and become better (iron sharpens iron)
- And yes, the ability for two parties to help each other reach new levels of success

That terrible period of time, immediately after losing Ethan, would have been infinitely more difficult if both Karen and I hadn't learned to appreciate the importance of meaningful relationships.

It's as if all of these lovely people with whom we shared time, love and care were sharing in our grief and thereby, alleviating some of the burden. No matter where you're at in life, you can start investing in others – all you need to do is turn to someone that you like, respect or trust and open your heart.

The power of connection will do the rest.

Your One Shot Lessons

Cultivating relationships isn't a science, but we can do so in meaningful ways. It's important to remember that:

- No-one that has ever achieved great success has done so without at least some help from someone else, so don't fall into the trap of thinking you have to do it all on your own.
- You are who you spend time with, so make sure the people around you are those you trust, like and respect. Maintaining these relationships requires ongoing effort.
- The three most important types of relationships in business are (i) those who share your mindset, (ii) those that can help you move forward, (iii) those who you can help move forward.

Things Do Not Happen To You, They Happen For You.

4

The Journey To Connect My Mind, Body & Spirit

"One of the most spiritual things you can do is embrace your humanity. Connect with those around you today. Say, 'I love you', 'I'm sorry', 'I appreciate you', 'I'm proud of you'... whatever you're feeling. Send random texts, write a cute note, embrace your truth and share it."

Steve Maraboli, Motivational Speaker & Author

I am sure that you can think back to a time when you thought you knew everything. Perhaps you were a stubborn 19-year-old who scoffed at older people trying to share some practical wisdom, because you had it all figured out.

Perhaps you were a cocky 25-year-old climbing the corporate ladder, who thought they understood what older generations didn't. No matter who you are or where you've come from, I'm sure you can remember a time when you inadvertently closed your mind to growth because you believed you were all the way grown up.

Of course, these are just broad examples. My case was a little different, yours probably was and is as well. In my early 20s, I purchased my gym and then ground away for 18 hours a day, in sink-or-swim survival mode.

Many of you may have been in similar positions. Some of you are right now. It may not be the fitness industry that you're working in, but if you are spending 50-60+ hours a week in any job or business, simply trying to hang onto what you have then yes, I know what you're going through. I thought I knew what it took to build a well-rounded life from the ground up but despite this, I didn't close my mind off to learning. I understood that progress required growth and growth required learning.

I ate up the wisdom of successful people. I read books and sought out mentors. I did all that I thought was necessary to get ahead in life. But where I fell down, was thinking that the only areas that required attention were health and wealth. Anything even remotely resembling spirituality wasn't on my radar.

It could have been that whole self-assurance thing. It's not unusual to default to a reliance on finance and fitness to see you through to your goals. In truth, they become the goal and therefore stop you from focusing on what you as a person really needs. Some forms of self-assurance can end up convincing you that whatever you've got right in front of you is all you will ever need. In my experience, that's simply not the case.

I continued in this fashion for many years. My mantra was "health and wealth for the ultimate lifestyle." When it came to health, I trained almost every day, so as to ensure my body was in the best possible condition. I ate all the right foods and took all the right supplements. Treating my body like a temple may well have been the closest I came to any kind of intentional spirituality to be honest.

When it came to wealth, I obsessed over growing the optimal mindset - one that would help me reach new levels of success every year. To me, keeping both of these dimensions in check was almost like an equation. You do x to achieve y and that should equal living the best possible life.

I thought I had it all figured out. And maybe I almost did, but it wasn't until later that I realised the value and importance of spirituality to me.

Then Ethan came… and left.

I Believe Spirituality Keeps Us Connected

After Ethan, I spent quite a bit of time attempting to process the tragedy. I was looking for a way that would allow me to move forward. This involved a lot of mental bargaining and questioning – of asking questions such as *"Why me?", "Why did this happen to us?".*

I wondered why there were so many unwanted pregnancies while Karen and I were given hope and then made to suffer disappointment and eventual tragedy. We were ready to give a child the best possible upbringing, a lovely home and the foundations on which to build a successful, happy life. And yet, WE were the ones who were made to go without children? Why?

Through this process of negotiation, I realised that I had been neglecting an aspect of life that was begging for attention. By placing such intense focus on health and wealth, on the mind and body, I had become closed off to a higher dimension – the spirit.

Spirituality is a deeply personal thing and it carries different meanings for everyone. I'm even hesitant to use the word because it can suggest everything from extreme dogma to a specific set of teachings or beliefs.

For me personally, I see it as a connection to something outside yourself that helps you become your best self – and that something can be anything from a god, to the universe, to the concept of a shared humanity.

There are many people who have influenced my spiritual side and I'm grateful for the mentors I've had along the way. I wouldn't say that I've subscribed wholly to one recognised discipline over another, but for me, spirituality has something to do with an unexplainable connection to Ethan. One that reminds me of what's important and helps me be my best self. It's a bond from here to somewhere that can never be broken.

Through the realisation that the unexplainable is just as important as health and wealth, I've been able to cultivate a strong feeling of (and derive power from) connection between myself and everything around me.

Today, I feed my mind, body, and spirit in equal measure. I know that I'll never be at a point where I have everything figured out – and that's okay. That doesn't mean to say we shouldn't strive for understanding…

7 Foundational Areas of Transformational Change

I have since begun looking at the trio of mind, body and spirit and how you can work to satisfy each dimension. In doing so, I ended up with **7 foundational elements** under the mind-body-spirit umbrella.

If tended to regularly with the ultimate goal of mastering each and every one, you can reach new levels of success in all areas of life.

The 7 foundational areas of transformational change

> **Health and fitness:** This one's fairly obvious, but encompasses optimising the body through a sensible diet, good nutrition (no it's not the same thing), mindfulness including meditation

and regular exercise (both cardio and strength training). Addressing this area not only ensures the body is functioning as best as it can and reduces the risk of disease, but it also helps to keep the mind in optimal condition – this will help approach the next six areas.

Personal growth path: Someone was telling me about a basketball coach telling his players that their careers are like a bowling ball halfway up a hill – if they're not actively pushing it, it'll roll backwards; if they simply lean on it, it'll go nowhere; and importantly, once you get it going, it's much easier to keep it going. It's simplistic but often these pictures serve as signposts or general instructions or even motivators. In short, be consistent, apply effort and don't ignore opportunities to become more.

Spiritual life: As above, I'm not talking about ascribing to any set of religious or spiritual teachings, but more about a connection to the unexplained; and an awareness of how that connection can help you become your ideal self and live life with purpose and passion.

Love life: Meeting a 'partner for life' isn't for everyone, but for many of us, committing to one person and forming a family together (however that might look to you) satisfies a human need for intimacy, companionship and mutual love and respect – and is often one of the many paths to genuine happiness. And where does that love thrive? In a home as opposed to a house, a mere building. I've learned that love is what transforms one to the other. That and a loving family.

Financial life: By this I mean achieving financial freedom, that is, earning the money required to not only survive, but live your desired life. But there's something else (there has to be, right?). Money is a means of creating something that lasts and lasts as a benefit to others. I'm talking about enduring memories and a legacy of impacting others – giving back where you can. That is the real power and definition of financial success.

Social life: Forming meaningful connections with people who bring out the best in you and vice versa; cultivating these relationships over years and becoming the kind of person who others want to be around and lean on.

Career/Work: Finding an occupation or vocation that directly aligns with your interests and passions and allowing your day-to-day work to reflect meaning and truth. Why is this important? Well, life is precious, we already know that. But what often gets overlooked is the fact that we spend huge chunks of it working. If you dislike what you do or it leaves you feeling empty, you're not living with passion or purpose. You are simply existing on this planet… until you're not. I want to inspire change - what do you really want to do?

The end result of the focus, effort and dedication you apply to these 7 areas is your **quality of life**. By consciously working on and balancing these 7 aspects of life, joy, happiness and fulfilment will be a part of everything you do and who you are.

If you're able to give each of these areas the attention they deserve, over time they will grow stronger and stronger. But a word of caution: balance really is the key here. If you're enjoying financial success and have your health but struggle to connect with anyone, you'll likewise struggle to find happiness.

Take any of the other components out of the equation and inevitably, happiness will be diminished. So, if you're able to keep that balance going, then I can guarantee that your life will improve in ways you never thought possible. You'll be well on your way to mastering the mind, body and spirit.

You Are Connected to the Universe

If the idea of an unexplainable force or higher power doesn't sit right with you, then perhaps think about your spirit in terms of the universe. I often say to people to open your mind and heart and look out for and lean into the signs. Exploring spirituality might not be for you, but keeping an open mind to it, is something we can all do with minimal effort or commitment.

What do I mean by the universe? Well, let me tell you a quick, true story.

My wife Karen's grandfather, David, was in his early 90s and struggling with poor health. He had expressed a wish that all he wanted was to live long enough to meet his first-born great grandchild. Sadly, in the weeks leading up to the tragedy with Ethan, Karen had learned that her grandfather was in his final days, so her mother rushed over to the UK to be by David's side.

In spite of what the doctors had predicted, David was still alive when we lost Ethan. He was bedridden and life was a struggle, but he was alive. Not only was Karen stricken with grief over losing Ethan, but she felt an additional layer of pain, knowing that her grandfather's last wish would not be granted. Or so it seemed.

Now, David's chances of living another week, let alone a month were slim at best. We had come to terms with the possibility of Karen losing her grandfather at any moment. Instead, David hung on not for a month, not for three months, but for over a year until Karen fell pregnant and delivered our first-born, Zachery. Not only that, but he clung to life for an additional six months until Karen and I were able to visit the UK with our newborn.

That's right, David was still alive, almost two years after we lost Ethan. That's almost two years past the moment that the doctors claimed would be his last. He received his final wish. He met Zachery and it was a fantastic moment and a memory that I'll never forget. The photo of the meeting is beautiful and one of my favourites.

David passed away peacefully, 12 hours after meeting his great-grandson Zachery.

I tell this story to highlight the fact that, sometimes, inexplicable forces are more powerful than any logic or reason. When Karen received the news that David was in his final days, all science suggested that he should have passed away.

His health was so poor that the chances of him living another two weeks were minimal at best, yet he defied all logic and reason and lived for another two years. I don't know how or why it happened, but I can't help but feel that the universe had his back.

Something outside rational explanation wanted him to have the chance to meet his great-grandson. Something gave him the strength to defy the odds.

The Guiding Path

I believe that things do not happen TO you, they happen FOR you. The universe is providing a guiding path and those challenges that arise and disrupt your life are there to help you navigate a new path.

Ethan, my greatest challenge, grounded me – it shook my very foundations and changed my attitudes towards everything. It made me consciously aware of being alive.

When you're consciously aware, you can use it to improve performance in business and in life. If you can really dive deep into the wisdom of operating from this place, your external life becomes an expression of your inner world. You can live with passion and purpose.

You can operate from love and gratitude rather than arrogance and competitiveness. You can strive for success from a place of empowerment rather than suffering. You can see the world around you with self-awareness, empathy and humility.

Now, part of me would love to say that I worked all this on my own. I suppose it is natural to want to find your own answers but that can't always be the case. Journeys are different for everyone; they feature meetings, both physical and of the minds, at different times for different reasons.

There have been a handful of people who influenced my own journey. The conclusions that these wise, generous and big-hearted people brought me to were invaluable. Their thoughts and principles on everything from healing to perspective to conscious wealth creation and their practicalities have resonated in many areas of my life and I am grateful for that.

To this day, I remain curious and continue to explore spirituality. Again, it's different for everyone, but I would certainly encourage anyone to simply lean in, listen to your intuition and be curious.

Now, prior to realising that there was a place in my life for the spiritual dimension, my drive for success was fuelled by something other than positivity – more like the desire to prove people wrong. My attitude was that I would win, because failure was not an option. After Ethan and becoming consciously aware, I operated from a place of love and gratitude. I was no longer driven primarily by money, but by meaning and legacy and impact.

Each of us possess a different relationship to spirituality. You can define it in any way that feels right. For me, spirituality is a connection to the universe, which is a connection to my best self. And I owe that newfound way of living and being – that discovery of the balance between mind, body and spirit that needs just as much attention as health and wealth – to Ethan.

Your One Shot Lessons

Mind, body and spirit form a powerful trio that can help you live with purpose and passion and it's important to put 'spirituality' in context:

- The 7 foundational areas of transformational change are 'health and fitness', 'personal growth', 'spiritual life', 'love life', 'financial life', 'social life', 'career/work' and 'overall quality of life'.

- If you give each of these areas the attention they deserve, over time each will be strengthened and you'll lead a more balanced life.

- Spirituality is different for everyone. A helpful way to see it is as a connection to your best self and as operating from a place of conscious awareness.

A Letter to Ethan

January 24, 2016

It is amazing how time flies and how things change.

January 24th is a very special day, because it is Ethan Schulze's birthday.

This time two years ago was easily the toughest day of my life watching Karen deliver our stillborn baby. Every minute of that day is still very clear in my mind.

The next phase was a whirlwind of grieving, funerals, and rebuilding your world that had just come crashing down.

After spending a few days in the presence of Ethan, I was at a crossroad. One direction is where you can blame the world. The other was the road I chose, and that was to take control and have Ethan as my inspiration.

Well two years have passed, and I am glad I chose the right path. In that time, my business went from good to great, we have our beautiful son Zachery Ethan Schulze, a new house, and I'm generally excited about the future.

I often sit back and think about Ethan and what could have been. He is such a special part of my life and, overall, he has made me a better person. My role now is to carry Ethan's inspiration and do my bit to make the world a better place.

Rest In Peace, little man.

You will be in my heart forever.

Challenges Are A Guarantee In Life. Put Each One Into Perspective.

5
Put Everything In Life Into Perspective

"Your reality is as you perceive it to be. So, it is true, that by altering this perception, we can alter our reality"

William Constantine, 17th century English politician

The day-to-day experience of living in this world can be tough. Stresses and setbacks come from all directions and sometimes it can seem as if you can't catch a break. I'm sure you've experienced a day where you've headed out into the world with a positive, motivated mindset, with a list of things you want to achieve and the intention to be your best and most inspired self.

Then, within an hour of leaving your doorstep, you've encountered unexpected traffic, maybe a particularly nasty fellow commuter and then perhaps, a curt or sarcastic greeting from a co-worker after being only a few minutes late. It doesn't matter what it was or what combination of incidents that may have taken place.

Suddenly, you're in a foul mood, your attitude towards seizing the day has been replaced with frustration towards everyone and everything around you and by the time you finish work, you've barely achieved anything on your list. A few more equally-frustrating days in a row and you begin waking up in the morning expecting the worst, all but guaranteeing the day *will* be worse. And the cycle continues.

That cycle is completely avoidable. On that first day, when you experienced the bad traffic, the nasty commuter and *that* co-worker, you could have seen events through different eyes. Instead of adopting the perspective that these things have taken place specifically to annoy you and ruin your day, you can reframe your perspective and acknowledge the events for what they are.

Traffic happens and you can use the time to breathe, focus and remind yourself of all that you plan to achieve. The nasty commuter has their own issues and who knows what's going on in their life - either way, their behaviour has very little to do with you. As for the co-worker, the reaction was small and unnecessary and should be dismissed as such.

Through the power of perspective, you can turn what threatens to become a bad day into the day you had imagined prior to heading off into the world. Catching yourself during an unproductive reaction and reframing your perspective in a way that benefits your peace of mind is an important skill to develop.

This shifting of perspective isn't only helpful during small inconveniences, but also when encountering larger setbacks, such as failing to get a promotion or writing off your car.

Kids See the World Differently to Us

Too often in life, we make unnecessary mountains of what are really molehills in the grand scheme of things. An undesirable event can seem disastrous until we place it alongside another of true heartbreak.

When we're children, there are no limits to possibility. Kids easily and confidently announce their desires to become doctors or astronauts or football stars and the concept of doubt doesn't even come into play. Then they grow up and move out of home and get a job and face a succession of challenges.

Whether it's debt and the stress attached to it, or ending up in a job they don't like, an unhappy marriage, or being saddled with a mortgage for the foreseeable future – life gets in the way. More often than not, this happens because they never learned a productive way to approach challenges. Let's focus on that now.

Tough Times Are Part of Life

"Every time you confront something painful, you are at a potentially important juncture in your life—you have the opportunity to choose healthy and painful truth or unhealthy but comfortable delusion."

Ray Dalio, Author of *Principles: Life and Work*

I've faced many a challenge over the course of my life. Growing up in an isolated town meant that at the age of 15, I had to travel 3-hours away just to find a school that offered year 11 and 12. Opening my first gym presented me with a steep learning curve that required complete, undivided and rigorous attention from the moment I woke up, to the moment I went to sleep, for months and months on end.

When I owned five gyms and went on my first holiday in years (with the intention to propose to my wife) and too quickly (and as I would later discover – foolishly) hired someone that wasn't up to the job of taking the reins, I lost almost half of my gym members and the business almost went under. Add to that, during the financial crisis, the health and fitness industry took a considerable hit and my bank reflected these uncertain times.

Were these challenges difficult? Yes. Did the global financial crisis of 2008 lead to cashflow issues that made paying the mortgage a problem and placed a strain on my relationship? Yes. Did I reach the point where I thought, 'This is too much'? I did. But with every challenge that I faced, I became more and more proficient in reframing my perspective of what they represented in the scheme of things.

That old saying that nothing is certain but "death and taxes" should be amended to "death, taxes and challenges". No matter who you are, where you grew up or how privileged your upbringing, you will, with all certainty, face challenges. So, if you know that they're definitely going to arise on a regular basis, then why not find a way to look at them as a natural part of life? You've only got one shot at it so, why not start cultivating a mindset that accepts, embraces and meets every challenge that arises?

How do you develop that mindset? You look at each challenge as a way to grow, to learn, to build resilience. You ensure that no matter how difficult a challenge might seem, you're taking at least one step towards moving forward each day. You realise that on the other side of a challenge there is hard-won strength and that each challenge you face with passion and purpose makes the next one that much easier to overcome.

And of course – you put that challenge in perspective. Yes, losing money, or a job, or breaking up with a partner, or failing at a pursuit are all difficult to negotiate. Yes, they're disappointing and painful and sometimes it seems easier just to give up. But are they life or death, or just a part of life? As Ray Dalio says, *"Painful junctures in life can be taken two ways. One is facing the truth. The other is fostering delusion".*

The truth, is seeing the challenge for what it is, accepting responsibility and finding a way to learn and move forward. The delusion, is failing to put the challenge in perspective, blowing it out of proportion and letting it destroy you, or placing blame on others or the world. If you work on developing the right mindset, then eventually, delusion won't even be an option.

Embrace the Challenges You Face

Over the last 20 years, I've worked hard to reach a position where I could travel all over the world and experience many different cultures. Through visiting places such as Africa, India and the Philippines, I've been exposed to ways of life that many western cultures couldn't even imagine.

From visiting small villages where residents are scraping for their next meal and struggling to find shelter, to impoverished areas where children as young as my own were forced to use public streets as bathrooms – the sobering realities of my relative privilege have become clear as day.

"You don't know how lucky you have it" is a cliché until you truly see it in practice. And seeing it, confronting it, then letting it sink in is another way to put your problems into perspective. These experiences not only gave me perspective but awakened the philanthropist in me.

Since then, I've been heavily involved in charitable endeavours and learned to not be so focused on my own concerns. I'd recommend that anyone and everyone with the means to travel and see how other cultures and people live, do that at some stage in their lives.

Some people might say: "It's okay for you or people like you, because you've had a level of success and you don't face the problems that I do". Perhaps that's true, but whether you're a multi-billionaire or someone gunning for an entry-level opportunity or anywhere in between, you all face challenges of the same nature, the only difference is how they present themselves.

A problem arising while overseeing 2,000 employees and one that arises while team-leading a handful of co-workers - or even one that you tackle as a sole trader - can be just as difficult, stressful (and just as surmountable) as each other.

Over the past five years, since the experience of losing Ethan, I've faced many a challenge both at work and at home. Every time one arises, I focus my mindset, channel my strength and remind myself, it's a natural part of life.

Then, I turn to my phone and take a moment to look at its desktop wallpaper – a picture of little Ethan's feet. I let the memory of that dark day put this day in perspective, remembering that the world is a beautiful place and opportunity is everywhere. Suddenly, the challenge doesn't seem so challenging.

Your One Shot Lessons

Without perspective, life becomes blurry. A sharper, more inclusive perspective can help you in a number of situations, in a number of ways.

- Perspective is a helpful tool that allows you to step outside a moment and assess it with objectivity by placing it in context of what is and isn't important.
- Challenges are a guaranteed part of life so being able to reframe your perspective each time you face a challenge, is an endlessly rewarding skill.
- Find a memory or moment that reminds you of what's *really* important, whether it's losing a loved one or the birth of your child or whatever illustrates the preciousness of life – and use it as your go-to mental image in times of challenge or even crisis.

Self-Awareness Will Save You From Your Ego Blindspot.

6

How To Get The Best Out Of Your Ego

"I believe that the biggest problem that humanity faces is an ego sensitivity to finding out whether one is right or wrong and identifying what one's strengths and weaknesses are."

Ray Dalio, Author of *Principles: Life and Work*

When we're young children, on the whole, we all operate with a similar mindset. One that is free, open and excitedly leaps at every opportunity. We aren't concerned with what other's think of us nor what we think of ourselves and that allows a deep, present connection to the world around us.

That said, there is a certain self-awareness, even at a very young age. From as young as six months old, there is a sense of ego, although it's a different version to the one we experience as adults. Ego in children is a feeling of 'separateness'. For example, your mother devotes an hour to day-to-day concerns while you play with your toys.

The idea that she isn't giving you undivided attention exactly when you want it can affect a child emotionally – toys may be thrown from the cot or play area, that sort of thing. It shows that even from a very young age, we feel entitled to possess the things around us, that may or may not belong to us. But in this case, all it leads to is a brief tantrum that (hopefully) leads to a hug. The real potential for damage that ego can have comes later.

Be Strong Enough to Admit Your Weaknesses

If you look at all the people you've met over the course of your life, chances are you've encountered a particular kind of person. The kind of person that no matter the situation, finds it impossible to admit to any wrongdoing, mistake or failure.

If they lose at a board game, they will find justifications as to why the outcome is unfair. If they are experiencing relationship issues, they will always place blame on the other person. If they are judged or graded and fail to come in first place, then the assessment process is rigged.

Pointing out someone's flaws who will never see them for themselves may be fruitless. In their mind, flaws are not an option. They are the best and most righteous and anything that challenges that fact is an issue.

This kind of mentality has a ripple effect on all areas of life. Professionally, it can strip you of all accountability and make you an impossible co-worker. Personally, it can push others away and erase the possibility of true connection. The irony is that the belief that you are simply cannot fail is almost a guarantee that you will end up failing – as you never capitalise on the opportunity to grow.

The ability to accept when you are wrong, when you've made a mistake, when you have room to learn and get better… is one of the keys to moving forward in life. In fact, honestly assessing your own actions and behaviours and admitting when you're wrong (or can or could've done better) can be disarming and even charming. I can guarantee that if you sat down with any of the most successful people on Earth and asked them to recount their life's story, they would discuss their failures just as much as their successes. In almost all cases, you can't have one without the other.

This downfall, if you like, of this "perfect" person can be summed up in three words: an unhealthy ego.

A Healthy vs Unhealthy Ego

There is a common misconception that having an ego means that you're arrogant and couldn't give two hoots about anyone but yourself, your needs and your image. That couldn't be further from the truth. Each and every one of us possesses an ego and it's an important, even a helpful attribute to possess – if it is handled in the right way.

In the business world, especially if you have entrepreneurial aspirations, ego is necessary. You need self-belief, the ability to envision a future of success and the lifestyle that comes with it. If somebody attempts to dissuade you from your dreams, to push you off your path, your ego can come in to save you – putting some steel into your spine and keeping your eye on the ultimate goal.

Sometimes, an ego requires you to be stern and unrelenting; to make difficult decisions – others may not like that. You may have to fire someone you like as a person but who is doing your business a disservice. Ego, in many ways, can be your saviour and it is vital to the pursuit of success.

But what helps regulate that? What helps you define and identify the areas you need to focus on, be sure of and hold firm to. Well, there is a word for that: self-awareness.

One of my all-time favourite entrepreneurs is Gary Vaynerchuk (many know him simply as Gary Vee) in part because of the stream of high-value content that he makes available to anyone who wants it. He is knowledgeable and generous with that content and many have benefited tremendously from his conversations – especially around self-awareness.

Without self-awareness, it's very difficult (if not impossible) to identify what you're very good at and by contrast, what you should ask others to do for you. Gary Vee has often suggested that if we, through the power of self-awareness, could focus more of our energy on what we know we're good at and less on what our ego tells us we should try and get good at, we'd be far better off. And finally, self-awareness points us towards self-belief, which is important.

But there's a difference between self-belief and self-importance. There is a difference between staying true to your opinions and perspectives and closing your ears to anyone who might offer valuable insight or constructive criticism. And that difference is easy to pin down – a healthy vs an unhealthy ego.

Millions of successful people have been destroyed by unhealthy egos. Take Jordan Belfort, the former stockbroker whose life formed the basis of Martin Scorsese's epic film *The Wolf of Wall Street* (2013) – definitely one of my favourites.

According to the movie, Belfort was a man with considerable business prowess. In his youth, he took a job as a door-to-door meat and seafood salesman. Within months, he was running multiple trucks and selling over 5,000 pounds of product per week. The margins, however, were too small and this particular venture tanked.

We are told that at the age of 27, Belfort founded Stratton Oakmont, a stockbroking boiler room that pushed worthless penny stocks on impressionable investors. Instead of putting his business potential to good use, the movie depicts an army of defrauders, making millions of dollars and living a lavish lifestyle that included parties, yachts and massive amounts of recreational drugs.

Despite his firm operating under near-constant scrutiny, Belfort's ego told him that he was smarter than the authorities and could keep them at bay while continuing to relieve people of their hard-earned money.

He had an uncanny ability to find loopholes and dodge punishment, to rouse the people around him with impassioned speeches and promises of wealth and glory and he believed that these abilities made him unstoppable.

Of course, karma/the universe/natural justice (you choose) caught up with him and his ego. In 1999, he was indicted for security fraud and money laundering and served 22 months of a four-year sentence in exchange for a plea deal. During his time in prison, Belfort took stock and cultivated a new attitude, learning a powerful lesson that he used as the basis of a successful career as a motivational speaker.

This is the prime example of what an unhealthy ego can do to a person. It's been concluded that Belfort let his sense of self inflate to such an extreme that he became entitled and deluded.

A healthy ego will help you reach and maintain success. An unhealthy ego will result in delusions of grandeur and a failure to accept the natural flow of life. When it came to Belfort's ego, he was plagued by a massive blind-spot, one that could only be remedied by honesty and integrity.

But these points are based on a movie interpretation that was wildly popular for a time at the movies. What about real life?

Well, during one of my podcast episodes on *The One Shot Movement Podcast*, I had the opportunity to speak directly with an inspirational keynote speaker, Marques Ogden. Having amassed some wealth doing what he loved for five years as an offensive lineman in the NFL (National Football League), Marcus started a business that quickly flourished into a multi-million-dollar enterprise.

However, seven years later, it all came crashing down with his involvement in a bad business deal and I was led to believe that Marques' ego may not have been an innocent bystander in this episode of his life. It was an expensive lesson in every sense of the word however, a stiff dose of self-awareness and perspective set this driven and inspirational man back on his feet.

The Key to a Healthy Ego

Apart from strength of character and a realistic perspective, the main factor that determines a healthy ego is remembering where you came from. Firstly, no matter who you are or what level of success you've achieved, you still have something in common with every other person on Earth – you are human.

Seeing yourself as separate or above or an exception to the rule flies in the face of logic and truth. When we remind ourselves of the fact that we all started out as children and that we all, deep down, are the same – it's far easier to stay grounded, show humility and avoid the traps of arrogance and self-involvement. I would hazard a guess that we've all heard the saying, "home is where the heart." Well home can also be where you started out.

As for me, I'm from Tasmania and very proud of it. I'm proud of my community and friends that I've known now for more than 30 years. I'm happy to say that a core group of us still manage to catch up annually (despite having chosen different paths in life), three decades on from when we met in kindergarten. That's where I come from and it helps keep me grounded.

Secondly, if you happen to achieve any level of success, it's important to remember that you came from a place that preceded that success. Accolades weren't always thrown at you, you weren't always able to afford assets from your own earned money and at some point, you couldn't have cared less about success, reputation and worth. Staying connected (at least mentally) to where you came from keeps you humble and is a ready source of perspective.

Thirdly, remember where you came from in a literal sense and therefore remember what matters. Your family, your friends – those who loved you and still love you no matter the car you're driving or the second house you're buying. Success is great, it can give you freedom and opportunity and experience and material possessions. But it can't give you real friendship, genuine care or unconditional love.

When you let your ego balloon out of control, the negative consequences are too many to name. When you use a healthy ego to your advantage and keep an eye out for potential blind spots, while always remembering where you came from and what matters – the sky's the limit. Just make sure that when you reach that sky, you keep your head out of the clouds.

Your One Shot Lessons

We all have an ego, but we can't just leave it to do its thing or an unhealthy ego can develop. Thankfully, there are ways that we can cultivate a healthy ego.

- Know there is no such thing as perfect. Admit flaws and mistakes and seize upon opportunities to grow.
- Self-awareness allows you to accept your strengths and weaknesses and know when to enlist the expertise of others.
- Remembering who you are, where you came from and the fact that we all start and end life in the same way, will help keep your ego in check.

A Letter to Ethan

January 24, 2017

January 24th is my most reflective day of the year as it is my Angel Ethan Schulze's birth date.

January 24th, 2014 is still crystal clear to me.

I can remember packing my bags the night before, getting ready for a four day holiday to Lorne. On the way there, Karen and I went in for a routine check-up at the 31 week mark of the pregnancy.

At the appointment, we were advised that our future baby did not have a heartbeat. A lot can happen in one week.

So, it went from 'life is great' to absolute rock-bottom in a matter of seconds. I remember nearly instantly vomiting when hearing the midwife explain that there was no heartbeat.

My mind was racing all over the place. But it was the next period that rattled me as we were advised that Karen was going to have to deliver the baby naturally, knowing the outcome. Karen showed incredible physical and mental strength through the next 24 hours and it certainly was an emotional rollercoaster.

From there, we were able to spend the next two days in Ethan's presence, which I have to say was quite empowering. It was at that time I made all my promises to Ethan about being a better person and giving life my best shot.

The following week was like an emotional rollercoaster preparing for a funeral, going through birth and death administration, and coming to terms with what was actually happening. It was also humbling to receive so much support from family, friends, work colleagues, neighbours and even from social networking contacts.

Everyone told me at the time that time heals wounds. Maybe that is true, but only if the individual takes responsibility. After grieving, I made the decision that Ethan will empower me to do great things. I always celebrate his presence, and I have many items of Ethan's that always gives me that inner smile.

The photo of his feet is my most precious memory of him that I carry as the background photo on my phone. So, if I have a tough day, I look at his feet and say to myself "It's okay, nothing has been tougher than January 24th, 2014 and I made it through that period". Then, I quickly accept the challenge and move on.

A lot has happened in the last three years. I guess sometimes you are challenged in life, and it is how you respond that can define your outcomes. Life is a journey, you control your ride, so make it a good one.

Love always,

The Schulze family

Learn How To Leverage Time, Money And Meaningful Relationships.

7
Leverage Is A Secret To Success

"A wise man will make more opportunities than he finds."

Francis Bacon, English philosopher

Thousands of books on business success have been published over the years and just as many skills, abilities and traits have been cited as the most necessary in order to achieve it.

Resilience, tenacity, assertiveness, foresight, vision, drive, ingenuity, calculated risk-taking, the ability to lead – and the list goes on and on (and on). If you were to place any successful person's life under the microscope, chances are they would possess most or all of these positive qualities.

However, there's one ability that often goes overlooked. One that creates opportunity on top of opportunity and offers benefit upon benefit.

One that without cultivating it early on and exerting over the course of my career, I wouldn't be anywhere near where I am today. And that is the ability to harness the power of leverage - or more specifically, to leverage time, money and relationships.

Leverage, in essence, is making use of a resource to multiply the benefits of that resource. Leveraging a period of time means that you're using time to make or free up more time. Leveraging a business relationship means that you are allowing that relationship to –in some way, shape or form– contribute to the continuity of your success. And leveraging money, of course means that you are using your money in a way that builds money on top of money.

To some, this might sound obvious, but in reality, leverage is a far more complex and multifaceted concept. Opportunities to use opportunity to create more opportunity are everywhere and they come in a wide variety of forms.

Leverage Your Time

Time is a finite resource. It's more valuable than money will ever be. You can always find ways to go out there and make more money, but no matter how clever or crafty you are, there is no way you will ever be able to make more time.

Yes, you can make better use of your time, you know, slice it up into more generous portions but the pie itself is not getting any bigger no matter what you do. What you can do, though, is find ways to optimise time so that it's not only more productive and rewarding, but also so you can get more time back. And when you get more time back, you have more room to spend time with loved ones, to increase your learning - and to experience all that life has to offer.

Too often, we make the mistake of valuing money over time. We settle for the same routine or put everything we have into business ventures, working ourselves into the ground just to make ends meet for most of the year, every year, until we retire. We leave ourselves no room for growth, for perspective - and we ignore that niggling voice in the back of our minds that whispers "surely it can be better than this?"

Well, it can. The good news is there are a multitude of ways to use leverage, so that instead of being a slave to time, you are making it work for you.

It Might Be Time To Fire Yourself

"I just want to be right—I don't care if the right answer comes from me."

– Ray Dalio

Many new business owners and entrepreneurs make the mistake of jumping into the deep end and instead of swimming, end up wasting years treading water and sometimes, sadly, find themselves at risk of drowning. They tell themselves that in order to gain credibility and make a business work, then "YOU have to do everything."

YOU have to fulfil every role and handle every task, whether or not it's within your capability. YOU have to be the butcher, the baker and the candlestick maker. Sure, this might be the truth in the initial conceptual stages of a venture, but if you continue seeing yourself as an island, you'll end up stranded.

Billionaire hedge fund manager, philanthropist and the 58th richest person (at the time of writing), Ray Dalio, has often spoken on this matter. I was lucky enough to discover Dalio early on in my career and he opened my eyes to the reality that the desire to do everything yourself is merely ego getting in the way of productivity. No person on Earth is able to do everything themselves effectively and all that striving to do so gives you is an inflated sense of self-worth and not much else to show for it.

The antidote to this potential downfall is to fire yourself, that is to say, to look at your skillset with brutal honesty and see where you will benefit from outside expertise. For example, I've never been the most technically minded person, so I fired myself from handling all tech and hired someone who lives and breathes it. Now, that side of my business is a well-oiled machine and the time I get back from outsourcing it, far outweighs the relatively minimal cost of doing so.

I've done the same for various aspects of my business and now focus on what I'm good at - sales and marketing. And because of that decision, I have that much more time to devote to family, friends, hobbies and leisure.

Learn to Leverage Your Money

This is one of the key strategies in the pursuit of freedom. If you can leverage money correctly, you also free up time. Working this out for yourself can be a dangerous game, so it is of the upmost importance that you learn how to properly leverage money by paying a good financial advisor or find a good mentor. Pro Tip: save this one for the pros as it is not worth the risk.

For me, I read book after book about business, including property development. I turned to the right advisors and asked the right questions. My initial strategy was to build a business (a gym) and generate cash flow, then use the cash flow to generate wealth through property. I still use this strategy 20 years later.

The process is hard work and it can be slow – there will always be peaks and troughs. But once you build momentum, your finances can grow exponentially. I spent an incredible 12 years in the fitness industry owning gyms and helping the brand EFM Health Clubs expand into Melbourne. I am really grateful for the relationships I developed and thankful to owner Matthew Lindblom for the opportunities.

But since moving away from the fitness industry and into eCommerce, I have spent over a decade leveraging the internet, social media and smartphone technology to amplify my business, cashflow and lifestyle. I am grateful to have partnered with Jeunesse Global and for its founders Randy Ray, Wendy Lewis and Scott Lewis.

Jeunesse is a billion-dollar brand that promotes innovative youth enhancement products in over 100 countries worldwide. So, it is a massive and far-reaching enterprise and yet, it's like a family. And so, I want to acknowledge the field leaders and people in corporate that I've had the privilege of working with who have partnered with me on so many lifechanging experiences.

While promoting Jeunesse Global's amazingly effective youth enhancement products online, I've helped hundreds of people all around the world earn a full-time income. This is not only a source of pride, but it means that from the moment I close my eyes at night to the moment I wake, people in India and Africa and South-East Asia are making money, not only for themselves, but also for me. I've leveraged my money so that money grows on top of money, it's the same principle I use to afford my family and I, a larger slice of the "time pie" I referred to earlier.

No matter how you end up leveraging your money, the idea is that the further down the path you travel, the less time and headspace you need to devote to making that money – and the more you're able to experience all that life has to offer. Great.

So that's time and money. Let's come back to relationships because, as you know, these create some of the most precious time we'll ever have – and genuine relationships aren't for sale and can never be bought.

Leveraging Relationships is Key to Building a Valuable Network

Earlier in this book, I spoke of the importance of meaningful relationships in business and in life. I revealed that a natural by-product of forming genuine connections is that both parties do all that they can to aid each other's happiness and happiness includes success.

I've stressed that just because a relationship can be of benefit to you, doesn't mean that you look at people as vessels for consumption. Assessing someone's worth based purely on how they can benefit you, only ever leads to both internal and external problems.

By the same token, there's absolutely nothing wrong with seeking out those from whom you can learn, or who occupy spaces that you covet – as long as you're transparent about your motives.

People, on the whole, like to feel as if they have influence and agency and if presented with someone driven and passionate, will often go out of their way to help. Of course, the more successful one gets, the more they will be approached by those looking for guidance and advice – so I make these distinctions within reason.

The Power of Mentors

'The Heroes Journey' is a classic story structure that most novels and films follow – and stage three of this journey is "meeting the mentor". The idea is that any hero that sets out on a quest, usually receives advice or motivation from someone with wisdom before fully committing to that quest. From Yoda in *Star Wars* to pretty much every martial arts movie from the Karate Kid through to Rocky, mentors are an integral part of stories as we know them.

Mentors are just as important in life as they are in stories, as they help you:

1. achieve clarity

2. increase knowledge
3. gain the motivation necessary for your journey

Leveraging a mentorship merely means seeking one out and soaking up all their knowledge and experience. Mentors can not only help to place you on the path to success and focus your attention on the target you need to hit, but steer you back onto that path when things become difficult, causing you to stray from the straight and narrow.

Remember, you only have one life, a finite amount of time which means that in most cases, you'll only have one opportunity to make the most of it all.

Your One Shot Lessons

Leverage is one of the most important principles of a success, yet it is often overlooked. When employed correctly, it can be one of your greatest assets.

- The three main types of leverage relate to: time, money and relationships. In each case, you are utilising something that, if leveraged effectively, will yield a significant return.

- Leveraging time may involve firing yourself from a task or job and outsourcing it to someone with the skills to address it more efficiently.

- Opportunities for leverage are everywhere and it's important to develop an eye for them.

Come From A Place Of Love And Gratitude.

8

Generosity & Gratitude Changes Everything

"Generosity is the best investment."

Diane von Fürstenberg, Fashion Mogul & Philanthropist

In my early 20s, I was full of beans and, when it came to business, a little green. Running my own gym was proving to be more than a full-time job, though that was on me, as I would spend most of my free time reading books written by the masters and getting as much insight as I could.

From the moment I woke up in the morning to the moment I shut my eyes at night, I lived and breathed all things business. But, it wasn't until I met Gary that things really started to fall into place.

The 8 Basketball Tickets That Changed My Life

One afternoon, a door-to-door sales rep entered my gym and asked whether or not I was interested in sponsoring a fundraiser for Adelaide's NBL (National Basketball League) team – the 36ers. While I wasn't yet in a position to put my money towards many charitable endeavours, I thought that getting involved in this event could maybe lead to some exposure for my gym. So, I donated a handful of 6-month gym memberships and left it at that, thinking nothing of it.

I'd all but forgotten about the donation when a month later, a lady came into the gym to claim her prize. We got talking and it turned out she was the wife of one of the Adelaide 36ers. She was lovely and gracious and thanked me for my support with eight tickets to her husband's next basketball game.

The tickets sat in the reception drawer for nearly a week, until a young family visited the gym and signed up as members. Instantly, we hit it off and I was so taken with the exchange that I, without thinking, surprised them with the basketball tickets.

I didn't know it then, but that single act of generosity would change my life forever.

Gary was the father in this family, and he became a firm fixture at my gym. As a thank you for the tickets, he invited me to join his family to their corporate box to watch the Adelaide Crows – the AFL team. Now, it's safe to say that I was an Aussie Rules tragic and I just couldn't believe my luck as we watched the match from this privileged vantage point. At least, at that point, I thought it was luck.

But it didn't end there. The family became corporate members of my gym and down the track, without prompting, they offered to let me use their corporate box for a gym function. I was able to offer members a reward for referrals that I otherwise would never have been able to offer. All of this generosity was fantastic and I was overwhelmed, but it was nothing compared to what was to come.

Gary and I quickly became close friends, despite the age difference. He ran charities, a not-for-profit and a large organisation and was an expert in both the stock market and the property industry.

Without a doubt, he had a great business mind and he could tell that I was young and hungry to learn as much as I could, as quickly as I could. So, he took me under his wing and proved to be a resource so valuable, you couldn't put a price on it. Without realising it, I had my first (unofficial) mentor.

When I was looking into buying my first property, Gary gave me a crash course in real estate. He went further than merely sharing wisdom or giving tips, he took me out into the field for practical experience.

I'd head over to his house and we'd sit down, pick out two or three properties then go out and inspect, analyse and review. What I learned from that experience was far more enriching and beneficial than anything I could have learned in a theory-based course. And it put me smack-bang in the middle of the road to success.

We've now been friends for over 15 years. Just recently, we went over the pros and cons of my newest property. I know that he enjoys seeing the fruits of his guidance and support just as much as I enjoy picking his brain.

That is as good an example of the power of relationships, mentorship, generosity and openness as I can conjure up. Happily, it's all true and even better, these kinds of occurrences happen all the time and if you remain open to it, they can happen for you too.

How to Make Waves Using the Ripple Effect

A single, unassuming act of generosity became a gift that kept on giving and continues to give to this day, like a small rock tossed in a pond that makes much more of a splash than its size suggested. I'm sure that if you scrutinised your life, you'd find at least one example of 'the ripple effect'.

Whether it's the series of seemingly inconsequential events that led up to you meeting your partner, or to you landing a job that ended up being far more rewarding than expected – we all benefit from (and unfortunately, are sometimes disadvantaged by) the ripples that result from small moments.

There are two morals to this story:

1. **Always keep your eyes peeled for opportunity**
2. **Give as much as you receive**

Number one is self-explanatory. It would be one thing for me to hand over the basketball tickets, meet Gary and then upon discovering his business prowess, remain quiet for fear of overstepping the line.

If I hadn't noticed that this was a man from whom I could learn and that his guidance could help me become a better business owner, then the ripples would have ceased there. It is one thing for a small moment to lead to larger moments quite naturally, but it's another thing altogether to capitalise on opportunities.

Number two is a common saying that many of us believe in but reserve for later on in life. It's easy to say, "I plan on being generous once I'm in a position to be generous". This kind of thinking is counterproductive and a little cynical.

Generosity comes in many forms and doesn't have to include parting with money or valuables. There's generosity of time and generosity of spirit. Lending an ear is generous. Complimenting someone is generous. Believing in someone is generous. Helping someone to move to a new house is generous.

If you go through life expecting and relying on the generosity of others without realising that others require that same kind of attention, then you run the risk of falling down in the long run.

Over the course of my career, I've cultivated an eye for people that need my attention - whether through companionship, advice and yes, eventually, financial support. If life is all about balance, then doing your part on the generosity front while accepting the generosity of others, keeps that balance in check.

What Will Your Legacy Be?

The older I get, the more I'm aware of the legacy I'll leave behind; of the impact I'll have on this world. I used to think that my legacy would be one of success and success alone, but it turns out that making a difference in the lives of others is not only just as rewarding but just as important.

A small part of Gary's legacy is that he helped me become the man and entrepreneur I am today. A small part of my legacy is that I'm writing this book to help others find some clarity and develop some tools that will help them take and make something more of their one shot at life.

Growing jaded, focusing on what's dark about the world and developing a negative mindset that sees no point in giving back to others is fairly common. The key to avoiding this attitude trap is to focus on what you can control and what you can control is your little corner of the world.

Instead of obsessing over what you don't have, perhaps start looking out for what you can do for those in your immediate vicinity. Ask someone if they're okay; ask them if they need anything. Tell someone that you understand what they are experiencing. If someone needs a helping hand for a few hours and you have nothing pressing on your plate, offer them that hand. Contribute to the world.

If someone is finding it difficult to make a decision, listen carefully and help them untangle their thoughts. Not so that one day you will get something in return (though with the way life works, you often will), but because it's how you would want others to treat you.

It might sound a little like a cliché, but as we all know, clichés became clichés for a reason – they're often made of truths.

Your One Shot Lessons

Generosity comes in many forms and nobody lives a full life without being on the giving and receiving end of it.

- If you have the means to help someone, do it. It will pay dividends in some way, shape or form.
- Spending your entire life receiving generosity without giving anything in return is a recipe for unhappiness.
- Generosity doesn't have to involve money or assets. There's generosity of time, of empathy and understanding and of spirit.

A Letter to Ethan

January 24, 2018

January 24th is a special day in my calendar as it is the day that I celebrate Angel Ethan Schulze's birthday.

There are events and circumstances that happen in your life that can define you and your direction.

I recently read that pain, whether it is physical or emotion, is the sign that there is reflection on the pain to learn and grow, then there is the evolution. Big lesson there :-)

January 24th, 2014 was one of those days. It was just a normal day and a few weeks to go before the arrival of Ethan, my wife and I had a simple routine check-up where no heartbeat was detected in our unborn child. I will never forget the midwife say those words.

To describe the next 24-48 hours is too hard, but my best description was I felt like it was an outer body experience. Emotions were crazy, thoughts were crazy, it was pure adrenaline. Then planning a funeral added another layer of emotion.

Throughout this experience there were many, many blessings. Number one is the value of relationships. When we arrived home, we had so much support from so many people. Flowers, home cooked meals, friends to talk things through, family, the Jeunesse family and extended networks all reaching out.

The spiritual side of my life was awakened. While that is very private and personal to me, it is an area of my life that I am deeply connected to.

I feel through Ethan that I have to keep moving forward to inspire people and leave a legacy, which is why I do what I do. Time is ticking and time stops for nobody. I have many projects sitting in the background that, one day, will come to fruition that will allow Ethan to leave a legacy too.

The 24th of January is the day I celebrate him through writing a Facebook post. I still keep his beautiful feet as the screensaver of my phone and, when I am having a tough day, I simply look at those feet and smile. Plus, we have many special memories of him throughout our house.

It has been four years but still feels like yesterday. Happy birthday, little man.

Deep love always xxx

Dream Big And Let The Magic Happen.

9
Your Vision is Vital to Your Success

"The empires of the future are empires of the mind."
Winston Churchill, former British Prime Minister

Here's a trajectory that millions of people end up following. Chances are you know someone who has, or maybe you have yourself.

Growing up, you were a dreamer. During your teenage years, you'd stare at the ceiling or into space and let your imagination run wild. As a young adult, train or bus commutes to and from work gave you a period of time for guilt-free daydreaming. You loved running possibilities through your mind – who you could end up becoming and how that would play out.

Maybe you imagined winning at business, carving out your own niche in a market that has always fired you up. Maybe you imagined kicking the winning goal at the AFL grand finals. Maybe you imagined meeting and tying the knot with the love of your life in the most elaborate and romantic fashion. Whatever the dream scenario, they were so enjoyable because of the feelings they manifested. Your ability to use your imagination to wonder 'what if?' was so powerful that the scenarios felt real.

Then, at some point, something changed. Instead of craving free time to dream, you began avoiding any tendency to do so. You became less open to possibility and more concerned with the fact that your dreams were becoming less and less possible. You shut off your imagination and saw your dream scenarios more as pipe dreams; reminders of the fact that you've never taken any steps to turn them into realities.

Dreams are important. But if you never learn that if you don't figure out ways to make them happen, then they remain dreams - and eventually broken ones. In other words, dreams are nothing without vision.

So, let's talk about the importance of a vision and the practical steps required in order to realise it.

Make a Plan For Your Success

If you were to interview anyone that has ever got ahead in life through their own efforts, chances are they will have, at some point, created a vision for the future. Sure, some people stumble into fleeting success, but most who have made something of themselves, have sat down, forged an image of their ideal future self and then figured out the steps required to make it a reality.

Whether you're a business owner or a CEO or a sportsperson or an actor, doing things on the fly without clear direction and expecting success, will almost never work.

Let's say you're a swimmer and you decide that you want to compete at an Olympic level, with the ultimate goal of winning a medal. Deciding on that end result is only the first step - you need to envision what's required in order to reach that level.

It's not enough to say, "I'll just train really hard". You need to find the right trainer and devise a step-by-step plan of attack. You need to say, "okay, this is where I'm at now and I need to be swimming at a certain speed by a certain date".

You need to focus on your diet, your sleep routine, your mindset. You need to set supplementary goals and incremental benchmarks. You need to compete at a local level, then a metropolitan level, then a state level, then a national level – and you need to know exactly what's required in order to move up that ladder.

Without vision, you're fumbling around in the dark and will most likely end up hitting a wall. And that may even come as a relief because by then, without a plan, you'll have realised how futile the whole idea was and be glad to see the end of that (mis)adventure. *That's* the importance of mapping out steps towards a vision.

Whether your ultimate goal is as grand as becoming an Olympian or simply to open a café in your local area that becomes a suburban icon (if not part of a chain…!), vision is of the utmost importance. And one of the most important aspects of vision is the ability to form positive habits.

Habits Are Your Best Friend

If someone were to ask you, "What are some of your habits?", the chances are you would attach negative connotations to the question. Watching too much television in the evening. Biting your fingernails. Eating too many sweets. We often think of habits as things that we need to stop doing, instead of the things we could do in order to live a better life. Positive habits are a successful person's best friend.

Imagine that you make the decision to lose 15kg in six months. And yes, I met plenty of people in my gym days that mentioned these sorts of goals as you can imagine. Setting that goal and thinking it'll be enough to get you there is a fool's game.

Your existing (bad) habits are already in full force and they are far more powerful than a decision that isn't backed by a plan. In order to reach that goal, you need to ask yourself "what will allow me to do that?", then create a series of new behaviours and repeat those behaviours again and again. The only way to eliminate bad habits is to replace them with new, positive habits.

So, for weight loss, you might decide to:

- exercise at least four times a week for an hour at a time
- choose exercises that increase lean muscle mass and help burn calories more efficiently

- cut out unhealthy foods and stop snacking
- drink more water

You then have to consciously decide to do each of those things, even if your mind and body show resistance (and chances are, they will). Once you make that conscious decision enough times, you'll find that you no longer have to do so – the behaviour will have become second nature and a habit will have formed.

Replacing ingrained, unhelpful patterns of behaviour with new, helpful habits is difficult. Even if you have broken down your vision into a step-by-step plan and figured out exactly which habits are required in order to reach your ultimate goal, chances are you may slip up on more than one occasion.

That's okay. That's human and it's part of the deal. As long as you reorient yourself and get back on the horse, you're still on the right path. It's important not to be too hard on yourself (but also not to go too easy on yourself either) and realise that it's all a process.

And if you need that extra hand…

Use a Work/Life Vision Book

Over my years of entrepreneurship and mentoring, I noticed that many people who wanted to improve the quality of their life and/or achieve something close to their heart, were having difficulty understanding how to go about it. I also met just as many who had settled for a life that didn't align with their passions and lived merely to make ends meet.

So, I decided to create a template to help people not only articulate their vision, but to discover it – and then map out the best way to make it a reality. I found that it has helped those that are stuck, find direction and those that have settled, uncover their spark.

Lifestyle by Design: Your Work/Life Vision Book is a short eBook that contains specific exercises that help you figure out what you want and how to go about getting it (also, feel free to stop by www.craigschulze.com for specific business lessons via my blog and if you value hearing views, tips and news from other world renowned entrepreneurs, you'll also find my podcast available to you on site).

It operates under the belief that no matter your vision for the future, happiness is the ultimate goal and the key ingredient to living a fulfilling and even extraordinary life. And the great thing about happiness? Once you get a taste of it, it breeds success. Show me a happy person and the chances are they will be living a full, well-rounded life.

Earlier in this book, I listed the 7 areas of foundational change. The idea was that when you consciously give each area the attention it deserves, you're on your way to designing the life and lifestyle you've always wanted. To recap, these areas are:

1. Health and fitness
2. Personal growth path
3. Spiritual life
4. Love life
5. Financial life
6. Social life
7. Career/work

In the eBook, you will divide your vision for the future into these seven areas. For each one, you assess its current state, imagine how you'd want it to change within a year, set an ultimate goal of where you want it to end up, then determine which habits and behaviours need cultivation in order to get there.

Other exercises in this eBook include writing a detailed description of your perfect day and brainstorming your bucket list. I also include a handy list of 20 life hacks to help you on your way.

It's Not Too Late to See Your Vision Fulfilled

> *"A vision is not just a picture of what could be; it is an appeal to our better selves, a call to become something more."*
>
> **Rosabeth Moss Kanter, Professor of Business, Harvard University**

The excuse, "I'm too old and set in my ways" is almost never true or acceptable. If you've always wanted to achieve financial independence, be in a band, succeed in business or get in shape physically, you can start right now.

Instead of spending every evening over the next five years wondering "what if", devote that time to learning and developing/practicing/working at it. You will be (pleasantly) surprised at how far you've come after five years.

Okay, so think back to an event from years ago - or even think about a favourite and shock yourself but looking up its year of production! The years literally fly by. If you're 30 years old and operating with the mindset that it's too late, then chances are you'll turn 35, then 40, then 50 and be in exactly the same position.

The fact that we can all learn new skills if we devise the right plan and **_commit_** (yes, in bold, underlined and italicised) to forming new habits is both exciting and freeing. "You can't teach an old dog new tricks" just isn't true.

Lastly, I want to make one thing clear: you deserve to be happy. If during this chapter, your thoughts have told you that there's no point in creating a vision because you a) won't be able to achieve it or b) you have made too many mistakes and don't deserve things to go right - then your thoughts are wrong. Remember, you are not your thoughts and you don't have to believe every thought as truth.

A thought is a sensation and is not permanent. If a strong breeze comes out of nowhere and you experience a slight chill, you can see it for what it is – a fleeting sensation. You can do the same to a doubtful thought – acknowledge it as a fleeting sensation that can pass without resulting in any lasting consequence.

The rest is up to you.

I can't wait to see what you do with a commitment to your vision.

Your One Shot Lessons

Success requires vision. Nobody who has ever achieved their dreams has done so without it.

- A vision requires seeing where you want to end up and articulating it as clearly as possible.
- Realising your vision requires breaking it down into steps and forming the necessary habits that will get you there.
- Contrary to what they tell you, it's never too late to form new, positive habits or create a new vision for the future.

The Magic Always Happens Outside Your Comfort Zone.

10

Take Action to Change Your Life

"A ship in a harbour is safe, but that's not what a ship is built for."

Unknown

Tell me if this sounds familiar. If it starts getting a little too real in the next couple of paragraphs, feel free to skip to the next action-packed section on taking action.

Here goes: you wake at 6:30am or thereabouts. You shower, brush your teeth, do your hair, get dressed. If there's enough time, you eat breakfast. You walk briskly to the bus or train station. You're forced to stand in a crammed compartment, sandwiched between other thrilled-to-be-here commuters. You grab a coffee on the way to the office. You spend eight hours on work that feels like bubble-gum for your mind, halved by a half-hour break for a lunch that's over before you even start eating.

You take another crammed bus or train home. If you are feeling up to it, you go to the gym. You cook dinner, eat it, wash the dishes. You prepare what needs to be prepared for the next day. You watch a few hours of television, barely registering what's going on, in and out of sleep. At 1:00am, you wake up on the couch and move to your bed. Rinse, rinse, repeat, repeat.

Maybe you exhale over the weekend but the stress of the work week stays with you up until mid-Sunday, when you finally feel a little more relaxed. Before you can fully feel it, the upcoming work week hits you like a semi-trailer and the stresses return before nightfall. You repeat this weekly pattern for 48 weeks of the year.

Some people love this, but many people that I've encountered, actually don't. If you don't… what are you doing?

In your head, you tell yourself that this isn't your life. It's merely temporary. Your real life will begin eventually and it'll be one where you're fully engaged. One where your days are filled with passion and purpose, where you are devoting your days to the pursuit of your dreams.

Where, if you so desired, you could head off to Japan for six months and work remotely

– while soaking up the culture and learning the language. Where you have the energy for adventure. Where you're someone that others come to for advice and direction. Where you smile and mean it.

The problem is that in most cases, this temporary life doesn't have an end point. You can tell yourself that the life of your dreams will happen eventually, without making a single decision or taking a single step towards making it come true. The stark reality is that in all likelihood, in another decade, you will still be crammed in the same train compartment, entertaining the same fantasy.

Unless of course, you take action.

Sometimes it can seem like everyone is living their dreams except for you. Yes, well that's simply not true. Remember what I said about clichés at the end of chapter 8? The majority of people are in exactly the same position; those that are living their dreams just get more exposure.

Most people end up settling for a less-than-desirable life while relegating their ideal future to fantasy. And the bad news is that more people go through life unfulfilled than fulfilled.

The good news is, you don't have to be one of those people. While everyone's dream is different and requires their own specific courses of action, there are a long list of universally-helpful steps you can take (and universally-unhelpful traps that you can avoid) that can set you on your way. Starting now.

Magic Happens Outside Your Comfort Zone

If you are walking through life like a zombie, the chances are your comfort zone is small in radius. You are probably feeling empty, unfulfilled or lost, and don't have a vision for the future or a passion or purpose for life. This comes with a huge cost.

Comfort is a word that is usually associated with positive connotations, like warm and safe. However, growth doesn't always happen there – and often, it's not where the magic happens.

Hundreds of quotes from great thinkers have been written about the importance of that area outside your comfort zone – for good reason. Any successful person will tell you that stepping outside that perimeter is where true living takes place.

Yes, it can be a place of fear, perhaps uncertainty, maybe a little anxiety. But if there's such a thing as the good kind of fear, uncertainty and anxiousness, outside your comfort zone is where you'll find it. Because when you confront them head on and come through the other side, you will be handsomely rewarded. Fun, joy, growth, stimulation, satisfaction and of course, fulfilment are all found outside your comfort zone.

This isn't to say that you should drop everything you're doing right now and do something completely radical. If you want to begin the process of knocking down the walls of your comfort zone and changing your life, don't just immediately quit your job.

It's all about starting a process, a journey, which can begin with something as simple as foregoing the few hours you spend zoned out in front of the TV during the evening and spending it on formulating a plan or vision, or working on something that aligns with your passions.

There are many successful people (and again Gary Vee comes to mind) that advocate devoting that "tv time" to working on your own brand of "hustle" so to speak. Primetime is called primetime because *so* many people decide to spend the hours between 7:00pm and 11:00pm or midnight or 1am or even 2:00am with their flatmate, the flatscreen.

Why not spend that time on working towards your dreams? The point is that you are confronting something that you've been avoiding for so long; something that will actually help you step back onto the path that leads to the life of your dreams.

Whatever your ideal future looks like, you can start working towards it right now. Do one thing every day that you've been avoiding, whether or not it scares you. In fact, if it scares you, it is probably exactly the thing you should be doing.

In time (and usually in a far shorter amount of time than you predict), that thing that brought about fear and uncertainty and anxiety will no longer feel that way at all. And as soon as you get to that point where you've entered the space outside your comfort zone, it's time to step further out.

Cynicism is Not Your Friend

I'm sure that at some stage over the course of your life, you've encountered someone who is defined by their cynicism. Someone who, perhaps, rebelled against anything positive and inspirational as a teenager, under the perception that it was cool (and perhaps because it got them laughs) and then never grew out of it.

Someone who then spent their life using cynicism as a crutch – sitting back, judging others and casting snide remarks so that they never actually had to take any chances. These people usually find that over time, their attitude sucks all the energy out of a room and pushes people away – and that the only people that remain are others with just as unproductive outlooks. It goes without saying that this way of viewing the world will never help anyone create the life of their dreams.

There's another kind of cynicism, though. A kind of 'selective' cynicism. Where you are supportive and encouraging and believing of other people's pursuits of happiness, but cynical towards your own. "I'll never be able to do that". "I'm such a screw up, so what's the point?" "I've made the wrong choices for too long and now it's too late".

It's bizarre that humans often fall into this tendency of treating themselves worse than they would ever treat someone else. If one of your close friends or family members came up to you and made any of these self-defeating claims, you'd tell them that they're wrong and do all that you could to motivate them, so why would you think you deserve any less?

The way many people are going, they are one bad day away from making cynicism a lifelong friend. Instead of starting the process of changing their lives for the better, they could easily begin to label themselves a failure and closing off their minds to growth and experience.

The Value of an Open Mind

The older we get, the more likely we are to close off our minds to change, when really, it should run the opposite way. Show me someone who, over the years, opens their mind further and further and I'll show you a life well lived. And the good news is that we all have the potential to knock down our mental walls just as much as we can knock down the walls that define our comfort zones. All you need to do is begin the process of letting things in.

Instead of devoting the evenings to switching off and pretending this isn't your life, you can devote those hours to picking up a new skill or rediscovering a dormant passion. Say, for instance, you always dreamed of being an illustrator for children's books. A few hours sketching away (even while watching television, if you must) each night, multiplied by a few months and you'll be amazed at how much you have to show for it.

You could buy books on illustration and soak up as much knowledge as possible. You could join forums. Email writers in search of collaboration. You could even contact successful illustrators and ask for advice.

Even if you don't receive a reply, you're starting up the engine. You're lighting the fire inside. So maybe drawing is not your thing. The same principles apply to developing or growing a business, a healthier physique or even mindset. Even with a full-time job, you'd be surprised how much you can achieve when devoting even an hour a day to a side project.

But nothing will ever happen if you don't take action.

The clock's ticking by the way… what are *you* going to do?

Your One Shot Lessons

Too often in life, we see our unsatisfying situations as temporary and tell ourselves that things will just change, 'one day', instead of doing something that will actually help – taking action.

- You can start taking action right now. Doing so requires nothing more than you making up your mind to do so.
- Achieving your dreams requires taking action in the areas outside your comfort zone, as that's where the magic happens.
- Cynicism and close-mindedness are a dream's worst enemy and are usually methods of self-protection. If either arise, make sure you have a counter argument ready.

A Letter to Ethan

January 24th 2019

January 24th is an extremely special day in my calendar. It is a day of reflection and empowerment. It is Angel Ethan Schulze's birthday.

Five years ago, was without doubt the toughest day of my life. Karen and I were getting close to being first-time parents and, deep into the pregnancy, we were advised that there was no heartbeat and that our soon-to-be son was to be delivered stillborn. Our lives changed forever that day.

Every year on the 24th on January, I get up in the morning and write a tribute piece in memory of Ethan to celebrate the day. Hopefully, someone reads the post, and it inspires them to create a positive change in their life.

This morning, I got up and read each post I have posted over the years including the raw original one (still feels like yesterday).

My favourite treasure I have of Ethan is a photo of his feet, which I still have as the screen saver on my phone. Whenever I have challenges, I always look at the photo and say to myself, "it will be okay". Over the last five years, I have certainly had to call on that photo a few times. Life is a journey and you are constantly navigating your way through challenges. Remember to just move one step forward every single day.

I look at that photo every single day as a beautiful reminder of the impact Ethan has had on my life.

It has been five years (where did that time go). Karen and I are now blessed with Zachery Ethan and Zoe Madison Schulze and it is absolutely joy and happiness watching them grow and change on a daily basis.

Over the last couple of months, I have been spending a lot of time listening to incredible personal development content about life. There was one interview that had a profound impact. It was all about LOVE, in both words and actions. It is so easy to say words like "I LOVE YOU".

However, true LOVE is actually best displayed by action. If you truly LOVE the person you are saying the words to, then give them a deep and meaningful hug at the same time. It does not have to be a hug it might be a beautiful message in a card or an action that displays your love.

On January 24th, 2014 losing Ethan opened me up to say the words "I LOVE YOU" a lot more. I now say it with real meaning.

Next time you walk into your house and say, "I love you" to your partner, kids, family and friends, show them you really mean it.

Love and Gratitude,

Craig D Schulze

Don't Be Pushed Around By
The Fears In Your Mind.
Be Led By The Dreams
In Your Heart.

11

Make Sure You Keep Your Dream Alive

"Dreams are illustrations... from the book your soul is writing about you."

Marsha Norman, American Playwright

For many of us, the smartphone is that black box with our lives (including some of our addictions) neatly arranged in files, folders and photos. It's the first thing we see upon waking and the last thing we see before sleep. It's the thing we turn to on the way to work, on the way home from work, in breaks from work and even during work.

If you're such a person who only uses their phone when necessary, more power to you, but for some, the smartphone can take the life out of life. It can take such control of your world that even when with friends and family, you're pulling it out every few minutes and flicking between apps without registering what you're looking at.

It can detach you from true human connection and make you impatient with the flow of reality. It can stop you from reading books, watching films, even from enjoying a sunset (unless it's a photo pushed through filters and posted to Instagram).

Sadly, for far too many, their best friends are apps, likes and follows, breaking tabloid news stories, comment threads, retweets, memes, gifs and games. These all distract from the fact that time is moving on regardless.

Don't get me wrong, modern technology is astounding and necessary and I wouldn't be where I am without leveraging online platforms. But if you're spending vast amounts of your discretionary time being unconsciously unproductive, are you really giving life your best shot?

I have a challenge for you. For one whole week, see if you can only use your phone when necessary in terms of engaging someone in a meaningful way or as a tool that will directly help you develop an aspect of your business or chosen pursuit. If you take the train to and from work, spend that time looking up and being engaged with your surroundings.

Instead of falling asleep scrolling through social media, pick up a book. If your instincts tell you to check your feeds, fight it. It doesn't have to be forever, but just see what happens over a week. Why? Because engaging with the wider world through personal experiences are always more relatable to real people – the people with whom you can build genuine relationships.

Too Many Distractions Equals Less Productivity

Why the challenge? Well, the modern world is littered with things that distract us from being in our own bodies. Whether it's mobile phones, or Netflix, or video games, or the drinking culture, or tabloid news, it's easy for us to fall under a spell that consumes our time and even takes over our lives. This has a number of detrimental effects on a person, but perhaps the most tragic is that it disconnects us from the pursuit of our dreams and slowly but surely destroys souls.

I've said it before, but I'll say it again – as humans, we are designed to dream. When we're young, dreaming about life's possibilities is a natural part of living. Nobody teaches us to dream, nobody tells us we have to dream. Children are more connected to their true selves than any other age group and a large part of that truth is a strong, ever-present relationship with the imagination.

What makes us stop dreaming? It's different for everyone. It could be the imposition of someone else's idea of what's possible (and impossible) for "someone like you.". It could be the first time you experienced significant failure. It could be the death of a loved one. It could be the stress of having to pay the bills. It could be society's obsession with 'getting old'.

If you happen to be that person that has stopped dreaming about the future and all its glorious possibilities, chances are you could run your finger back along the timeline and pinpoint a moment that closed the door on the good kind of imagination.

If there's such a thing as the good kind of imagination, then there's such a thing as the bad kind. In a recent study conducted by the Australian Bureau of Statistics, more than 2.5 million Australians suffer from anxiety. Of course, there are many causes of anxiety, but in many cases, I see it as your imagination going in the wrong direction.

Instead of imagining the good that can come, you spend your time entertaining all of the bad scenarios that most likely will never take place. Remember, fear actually destroys dreams and if you no longer have dreams… If you are such a person that spends all their time worrying about what might go wrong in the future, what would happen if you instead spent that time and headspace imagining what could go right?

You often hear parents say that one of the best things about raising a child is seeing things through young eyes. There's an infectious joy to seeing a child get lost in their imagination. If a child wants to ride in a rocket ship, all they need is a few pillows and their imagination. If a child wants to be a doctor, all they need is a plastic stethoscope and their imagination. If a child wants to be Superman, all they need is outstretched arms and their imagination. In their mind, they're already wearing a cape.

If you really want to design the life of your dreams, don't lose that Superman cape. If you have lost it, you can always find it again… but it may not be on your phone. Make sure you make time to look around.

One Moment In Time Can Change Everything

If you have stopped dreaming, or you've become accustomed to silencing that voice that's crying out to dream, then I have some good news: you can change. The older we get, the more we tell ourselves that any significant change is too difficult. That we are too set in our ways. Too detached from the person we always wanted to become.

If you have been working a job that only ticks one box, five days a week for over a decade and you don't have any significant training or skills in other areas, it's easy to shrug your shoulders, sigh and say, "Well, change is too hard and it will take too long". In reality, your whole life can change in second.

Consider those that have encountered near-death experiences. Someone is bushwalking and loses their footing on a mountain ridge and nearly plummets to their death. Someone loses control of their car and crashes, their empty passenger seat crushed by a telegraph pole. A steel beam falls and barely misses the head of someone working on a construction site.

In almost all cases, you will find that these people adopt a completely new outlook on life in an instant. They are the same physical being that they were before and after the life-changing experience. But in a brief moment, they realise the fragility of life and get their priorities in order.

I experienced some version of that moment when my son Ethan passed.

The point is, you can disrupt your brain's patterned thinking in an instant. You can make a choice to start listening to the voice inside you that is crying out to dream. You can start looking forward to what may come rather than dreading what will probably never happen.

Yes, hard work, dedication, direction and focus are all required, but consciously deciding to open your mind up to dreaming is a huge step and should never be underestimated.

That moment, that wake-up call that can happen in an instant, can set you free.

Turn Your Dreams Into Reality

Great. What a relief, it's not too late. But how? Well, achieving your dreams requires a blend of child-like imagination and adult rationality. If you're 35 years of age and you have made the conscious choice to finally listen to your dream of becoming an elite football player, you can't just knock on the door of your local team's training facility and say "I've just decided that my dream is to play for you guys, put me in the line-up".

Lying in bed at night and imagining what it would be like to score for your team is one thing (and an important thing, as visualisation of the end goal is a fantastic way of staying motivated and on track) but turning that scenario into a reality is another.

In reality, the journey probably starts with making an honest assessment of where you are physically and ability-wise. At say, 35, this could be quite confronting – maybe. You need to acknowledge the fact that you won't be brilliant overnight and that there'll be days where you struggle, where you fail, where you are plagued with self-doubt.

But as long as you keep your eyes on the dream and remind yourself of the peaks and valleys that every single successful person has faced on the way to achieving their goals, then you're in the best possible shape.

Whatever your pursuit, aim or goal, it's not going to be as easy as it was in your dream. Reality rarely is.

Wait! I haven't mentioned cold hard reality yet.

Okay, here are some facts. There are just six of them, but between us, we could probably come up with 30 inside the next 60 seconds:

1. Professional athletes, musicians, gamechangers usually get started in serious training and development by their early teens
2. Hamstrings are past their prime by the time you hit your mid 30s
3. If you don't have capital or access to capital today, you probably can't employ 10 people in your start-up tomorrow
4. Experience takes time
5. Expertise usually comes with experience
6. Good mentors make for easier development, but they can be hard to find… at first

Okay, what was all that about? It was about the need to dream big but create realistic goals while setting milestones along the way. You've heard this before, but it is worth repeating – often. You might love sports (and I most certainly do) and have dreams of creating memorable moments in huge stadiums in front of ecstatic fans. But be prepared to do the hard yards, set milestones, work smarter and stay focused on the dream.

So realistically, what are the chances of putting in a top performance in a footy grand final? Well, how about the odds of creating a business and beautiful life for your family when your one shot at that life hinged on leaving town to finish high school?

The combination of balance, hard work, drive, ambition and realism is the only way you'll even come close. Will you make it? The smart money may say no. But what did the smart money say about that kid from Queenstown riding his BMX bike to the lake?

Don't put it off any longer. Make the conscious decision to start listening to your inner-dreamer and know that you deserve to dream.

The human mind is an extremely powerful thing. When utilised properly, it can do amazing things. In other words, you can do amazing things, as long as you never stop dreaming.

Your One Shot Lessons

The older we get, the more likely our dreams fade into the background. Don't let that happen.

- The modern world is littered with distractions and time-wasters that take us away from our dreams. Make a conscious effort to imagine what you really want; what would really make you happy.
- Allowing yourself to dream without judgement or cynicism opens you up to life's possibilities, energises you and gives you a sense of purpose.
- Worrying about the things that could go wrong is a waste of time. Imagining how they might go right, then setting realistic goals, is time well spent.

Live Your Life With Passion And Purpose.

12

You Only Get One Shot at Life

"Life is an opportunity, benefit from it. Life is beauty, admire it. Life is a dream, realise it. Life is a challenge, meet it. Life is a duty, complete it. Life is a game, play it. Life is a promise, fulfil it. Life is sorrow, overcome it. Life is a song, sing it. Life is a struggle, accept it. Life is a tragedy, confront it. Life is an adventure, dare it. Life is luck, make it. Life is too precious, do not destroy it. Life is life, fight for it."

Mother Theresa

In 2006, tennis legend Andre Agassi revealed that he hated tennis. Not only that he hated it, but hated it with a "dark and secret passion". The US superstar sent shockwaves through the sporting world and stunned his many fans. *Open*, Agassi's riveting autobiography, reached No. 1 on the *New York Times* Best Seller list and listed on *Esquire's* "The 30 Best Sports Books Ever Written".

Why would such a fantastic competitor hate the sport in which he competed for two decades? Why would he cast such disparagements on a career that gave him what many of us can only dream of receiving? What could be even remotely bad about travelling the world, making millions surrounded by adoring fans, living in luxury and being able to afford to do anything one's heart desires?

The physical and mental toll that came with being one of the best athletes, hit Agassi more than perhaps any other tennis player in history. First off, from a very young age, tennis was forced upon him. Agassi's father was a relentless disciplinarian who transferred his dreams of tennis stardom to his younger, more malleable son. According to Agassi Sr., if his young son hit a million tennis balls a year, he would become great. He was right, if measuring a man by his resume.

But the truth was, Agassi wasn't pursuing his own dream, he was pursuing someone else's. After winning a Grand Slam title (one of the four, highly coveted major tournaments of the year), he called his father only to be told "you had no business losing that fourth set". He hated training, he hated competing and yet because this pressure to win was implanted in his brain from such a young age, he couldn't stop.

He couldn't stop when diagnosed with degenerative disc disease, a form of back pain that required cortisone injections that would eventually stop working. He couldn't stop when life as a tennis star interfered with his personal relationships and disconnected him from living life. He couldn't stop despite decades of depression and self-hate. He couldn't stop, even when he began self-medicating with crystal meth (methamphetamine) to feel positive feelings.

During the second half of his career and in the years since his 2006 retirement, Agassi became heavily involved in philanthropy, with particular focus on education. He created the Andre Agassi Foundation and in 2001, opened the Andre Agassi College Preparatory Academy, a public charter school that offers first-class education for K-12 students, preparing them for college and beyond. Agassi has said of this work that it is has been fulfilling in a way that tennis never was.

Be Patient and Enjoy the Journey

Agassi is living proof that the process is just as, if not more important, than the end product. The reason that every tournament win, trophy, paycheque and No. 1 ranking failed to deliver true satisfaction or joy is because they couldn't compensate for all that time he had spent doing something that made him miserable.

For Agassi, pursuing the dream his father had forced upon him was never the thing that made him happy, yet he continued to pursue it in the hope that one more win would change that. It never did.

The product, or result, or reward means nothing if the journey means nothing. Throughout our lives, most of our time is spent on the journey, not on the reaping of the reward, so it's imperative that we do all that we can to learn to love the journey – and that includes finding a purpose that directly aligns with your passion.

This isn't to say that the journey needs to be all roses. Far from it. Challenges, setbacks, failures and tough times are always going to come in to play. Some days you'll take two steps forward and one step back and other days you'll take one step forward and two steps back.

The goal is not to create a life where every minute of every day is perfect, but to find what it is in life that, on the whole, you love doing.

When you find something that you love doing, it's rarely a drag. You're not doing it because you have to do it, but because you want to. I wrote this book because inspiring people to live with passion and purpose lights me up. Having a hand in helping people to grow and evolve into the very best version of themselves is my why – the why behind this book.

So, feeling something similar for what you are working on means that you no longer have to live for the weekends or the holidays. You no longer have to spend 90% of your year counting down the minutes for that glorious 10% of freedom. Instead, freedom is found in the journey, not in the breaks from it.

Every Stage of Life Requires More Growth

Life is a compounding experience. The journey isn't a static thing, it's constantly shifting. The ideal journey has an upward trajectory. When you find that thing that you love and turn it into your life's work, you'll naturally want to keep growing and improving and building on what already exists. Achieving something and then standing still is a recipe for dissatisfaction.

When you reach each new stage of that upward trajectory, in order to move forward, a new you will be required. No, I'm not suggesting that you need to overhaul your personality or change who you are inside.

What I mean is that new skillsets and mindsets will need to be developed. The "five-figure" you, can't maintain a six-figure income. The six-figure you, can't maintain a seven-figure income. A team leader's mindset isn't fit for a manager. A manager's mindset isn't fit for a CEO. And so on, and so on.

Similarly, if you love being a parent and your ultimate goal is to become the best parent that you can be – that'll never happen if you aren't able to shift mindsets. You can't parent a teenager with the same mindset that guides you as you parent a toddler.

You can't be a parent to an adult with the same mindset with which you parent a teenager. In order to achieve what you want to achieve and become that ideal parent – you need to learn new skills and ways of thinking at multiple points along the way.

Part of embracing the journey is working on your flexibility. Knowing in advance that each stage of your life will require a shifting of mindset is empowering - even exciting. As long as you stick to your vision and acknowledge the fact that everything is constantly evolving, then you're in good shape. Your future will thank you for it.

You've Only Got One Shot

If you are reading this and the thought of following your passion conjures up feelings of fear and doubt - chances are it's exactly the thing that you should do. You should also take comfort in the fact that anyone who has ever been lucky enough to live with purpose and passion has experienced those same feelings.

Have you ever noticed that many of those in their twilight years suddenly develop a sense of honesty and irrepressibility that was lacking in their earlier adult life? They rediscover hobbies, do more of what they enjoy and express themselves without worry or fear.

Usually, this is because they've cottoned onto the fact that life is precious and they're in the home stretch, so why not be the truest version of themselves as possible? By the same token, how many people in that same demographic have you met who have claimed "oh, if only I had the chance to do it all again… if only I was your age… if only I realised x and y earlier…"

Why do we wait until the final phase of our lives to value the journey? No matter what age you are, whether you're 85 or 25, your days are numbered, so they should be treated with the respect they deserve.

I am living proof that you do not have to wait until the end of the journey to discover its preciousness. Since the tragedy with Ethan, I have listened to the callings of my truest self and let passion and purpose drive every single thing that I do, each day, every day, no matter the time, place or occasion. And you can too.

Whoever you are. Whatever you're doing in life. Whether you're near the beginning of the journey, or in or past the middle, you can start living the life you've always wanted. Nobody is going to give it to you. Nobody is going to tell you what it looks like. Because nobody is you. You are a unique individual with a unique perspective and you can discover and harness your uniqueness to create something truly meaningful.

Never settle for average. Never throw in the towel and let doubt, fear or negativity take the wheel.

Never let anyone tell you that you can't achieve what you want to achieve.

You can start living with passion and purpose right now. As soon as you close this book. You get out a notepad, listen to your gut and start writing down exactly what you want. Pin it to the wall. Highlight it. Underline it. Shine a desk lamp on it. Whatever you need to do to remind yourself of what's important.

You've only got one shot, so look inside and then look out to the world.

Your One Shot Lessons

You only get one shot at life, so you may as well go out and give it your all. For extra inspiration, keep the following in mind:

- You don't have to live the life you think your family, or friends, or societal norms, suggest you should live. You are the only one who knows what shot is worth taking.
- Figure out what it is that you love doing and put your entire being into pursuing that love.
- Don't wait until your twilight years to realise the preciousness of life. You can face the truth right now. You can start living with passion and purpose immediately. As soon as you close this book.

Conclusion

Success is a word that gets thrown around an awful lot these days and that's not necessarily a bad thing - far from it. But, like many good things in life, it can be corrupted if one facet is focused to the detriment of other aspects. Some people think only in terms of net worth. That sizes up their whole goal. Others focus exclusively on feelings or a singular accomplishment.

Many of us have come to realise that life is a collage or puzzle where the true beauty of the picture is not revealed until you've lived *all* the pieces of the puzzle. Relationships, gratitude, accomplishments, financial security, breadth of experiences, health… the list goes on. It all counts towards success and the big realisation comes when it becomes clear that you've only got one shot at getting it right - whatever right means to you.

Some of you will have realised that a lot of this book speaks to success in business. Good. I agree and I hope that if you have aspirations of finding success in business, I truly hope this book helps guide you along that path. In saying that, I want to make it clear that expressing and experiencing the full spectrum of emotion and gaining something positive from that, is also very much part of this book.

There's a tendency in our culture to see vulnerability as a weakness. Oh, he's too emotional. Oh, she wears her heart on her sleeve. Oh, they're both too fragile to be dependable. You'll often find that those who make these kinds of claims are the ones who, behind closed doors, are the most vulnerable and through some form of conditioning, have been taught that honest self-expression isn't a good thing.

My experience with losing Ethan and how that changed my entire attitude towards vulnerability is probably the best lesson I've ever learned. Without it, this movement wouldn't exist. When you're truly tapped into One Shot, when you see somebody that is able to open their heart and speak their emotional truth, you will feel inspired and connected, rather than judgemental and embarrassed.

Conclusion

The idea that personal or professional success can only be achieved by being tough and ruthless or confident and charming is not only a myth, but an outright lie. The more you acknowledge that you're a complex, living human being, the more you'll feel like one. That's called feeling alive. Truly alive.

The world is an unpredictable place. There's no such thing as a straight line to the realisation of your dreams. An endless list of factors come in to play, many of them out of your control. Knowing that you've only got one shot is one thing, but realising that once you begin giving it your best shot, things will almost certainly not go exactly as planned, is another.

Which is why you must remember that One Shot has nothing to do with being perfect or living life perfectly. One Shot is in the doing, not in the winning. Nobody can do the right thing in the right way at the right time, all the time. If we could, then life would be incredibly mundane. When you're really tapped into the spirit of One Shot, then there's no such thing as failure, only feedback.

Another important aspect of the movement is that nobody on this Earth knows what your particular One Shot looks like, but you. Letting the expectations or opinions of others dictate your way of going out there and giving it your best shot, means you'll more than likely end up giving it someone else's best shot – which never ends well, because it's not coming from a truthful place.

You hold the key to living with passion and purpose, to achieving success, to experiencing happiness. And when you're truly locked into that self-driven gear, then external validation and outside opinion no longer holds power over you. You can take it, do something with it, or leave it. You become unstoppable, no matter how many stoppages you encounter along the way.

An honest, unwavering sense of self that values the journey over the destination, that respects the doing over the getting, that isn't afraid to be vulnerable and encourage vulnerability – is a wonderful thing. It's the kind of thing that can change, has changed and always will change the world.

So, let it change yours.

This is it. Are you ready?

Letter to Ethan

January 24th 2020

Six years ago today, we lost my son Ethan who was stillborn.

Every moment from those horrifying words, "There is no heartbeat," right through to speaking at his funeral are still as vivid as if it was yesterday.

Ethan is in our lives in a different way. He drives my emotions in an empowering way. We talk about him all the time, and Zachery now refers to his brother. Today, he asked where his birthday party was going to be.

Every year, I have spent the day reflecting, journaling and putting together a tribute piece that people can be uplifted by. It takes me hours and hours and I probably edit it five times as there is so much I want to say.

Today's tribute is the day I bring Ethan's message, story, and legacy to the world as I said I would all the way back at his funeral where I said I will make him proud.

Ethan, this year I am writing a letter to you about how you changed my life, and why you are leaving a legacy.

"Dear Ethan,

Today we are celebrating your 6th birthday. It still feels like yesterday that we lost you. When somebody asks about the devastation, my best description is that the world stopped still, and it was like an out of body experience when you are put into a situation that you do not want to happen but you are forced to face the reality.

Ethan, you were my awakening and taught me more in one week about life than the previous 35 years. You were the greatest adversity in my life, but you have also become my biggest blessing. On that day my vision, mission, values, legacy, impact, and purpose all became crystal clear from that heartbreaking experience.

You taught me to be in the moment and outwardly love, listen, and have special conversations with your brother and sister. When these unfortunate challenges arise in life, you have two choices and that is to give up or rise up. You empowered me to rise up and share a powerful message with the world.

In the days after we lost you, I was journaling my feelings, emotions, and lessons I can carry forward.

At your funeral, I verbalized my feelings and I made a promise that I would leave a legacy in your name and that you would be proud. Five years later, I partnered with a publisher to make sure I followed through with my promise.

On your 6th birthday and from this day forward, I will shout this message to the world. That message is you've got one shot at life, so go out there and give it your best shot, live with passion and purpose and with absolutely no regrets. It is an absolute miracle to be born and to have your first breath, so make sure you give it your best until your last breath. It still saddens me that you did not even get one breath.

Losing you grounded me, humbled me, connected me to my emotions, and it put everything in life into perspective. I still have your feet on my phone and when I go through a challenge, I simply look at your feet and smile. You simply have allowed me to appreciate the small things in life.

Ethan, the vision and mission start now. You know that I will work hard on the ground, sharing the story and inspiring people to give life their best shot. You need to be the spirit guide that leads me in the right direction to connect with the right people and together we will create a global movement.

Love Always
Dad

P.S. The One Shot Movement is aimed to inspire people to move from adversity and challenge to be able to rise again. But also, people who are looking to take their life to the next level and become extraordinary.

We are launching a book that is raw, authentic, and vulnerable but at the same time highly educational with powerful lessons to thrive in life. The podcasts are interviews that are deep conversations with people to help inspire and educate, and our social media is set up to create a community and movement where like-minded people are empowered to give life their best shot whatever that is for them.

Our vision, mission, and values are to inspire you to live with passion and purpose whatever that is for you.

Acknowledgements

I would first like to acknowledge my wife Karen, who showed incredible courage and remained unbelievably strong through losing Ethan. From the moment we heard those dreaded words "There is no heartbeat and Karen will have to deliver this baby," Karen stayed in control and after the tragedy and the funeral, she was unbelievably determined to bring happy, healthy children into the world and give us the opportunity to be loving parents.

Karen is an inspiring mother who is loved by everyone she connects with and is extremely passionate and supportive about me sharing the message of our precious boy, Ethan. Karen, I love you with all my heart.

To my beautiful children Zachery and Zoe who bring joy and happiness to my life every single day.

During the time of the challenge and adversity, I would like to thank all of our family, friends, business colleagues and networks as the support, the conversations and the encouragement made a huge difference in our ability to move forward in a positive way. We are very lucky to have so many beautiful people in our lives.

I would like to thank all the incredible people from The Royal Women's Hospital in Melbourne that were involved in the pregnancies of Ethan, Zachery and Zoe. In particular, Professor Shaun Brennecke, who was such a guiding voice after losing Ethan.

I started journaling this story from the raw moments leaving the hospital up until the funeral. My heart spilled and I promised Ethan at his funeral that one day I would bring his story to the world. It took five years to start the journey, but I was encouraged by Johnnie Cass (Jack Delosa's Elevate Coach) who gave me the nudge to focus on making this project happen. Jack Delosa and all his team at the Entourage have been an incredibly empowering group of people to be involved with over the last few years.

I have to acknowledge Marlon Forrester and his team at Line & Length, for working with me on constructing the content for the book. Marlon and I have worked together on a number of projects and so we teamed up to put my words into an elegant read for the audience.

Acknowledgements

I want to give a huge acknowledgment to Emily Gowor. When I made the decision that I was going to commit to putting this book together, I wanted to get an experienced publisher involved, to ensure I delivered a world-class book. My first conversation with Emily was to discuss the vision and to explore whether my story was worth me investing the time, effort, heart and soul into the project.

From day one, we had an instant connection and she has guided me through the process every step of the way, from the mastermind at the start, all the way to delivery. Emily was incredible to work with. She put her heart into every step of the process, and I am forever grateful and blessed that we were able to work together throughout the process.

Finally, to Ethan, who is the inspiration for this book. The day we lost Ethan was a day that changed everything for me. His passing turned my world upside down, giving me my greatest challenge. But then he inspired me to be a better person.

I promised Ethan in hospital that I would make him proud and that we would leave a legacy together. He is the stolen heartbeat that allowed me to grow and live a meaningful life and I was blessed to spend those few days in his presence.

About the Author

Craig Schulze is a global leader, author, and renowned entrepreneur.

He has built many successful businesses from scratch and has remained a source of inspiration to thousands of people around the world. His focus and commitment to his vision have allowed him to build his dream lifestyle, by building businesses and making smart investments.

Craig is a multi-award-winning fitness professional. He travels the world as a speaker and coach. He is also a podcast host who has interviewed some of the biggest entrepreneurs in the world and is now launching his passion project, his first book.

Most importantly, he is a loving husband, a father and friend who loves to experience what the world has to offer and has travelled to over 120 cities around the world.

His vision, mission, and values are to give back through both inspiration and education through his one-shot movement. The one-shot movement is an inspiring message to live with passion and purpose as you only have one shot at life. In his final words to Ethan during the eulogy, Craig shared that he would carry this legacy forward, which he is now, the movement all about making an impact and a difference in the world.

www.craigschulze.com

www.ingramcontent.com/pod-product-compliance
Lightning Source LLC
Chambersburg PA
CBHW051537010526
44107CB00064B/2751